THE SONG AT YOUR BACKDOOR

JOSEPH HORGAN

The Collins Press

FIRST PUBLISHED IN 2010 BY
The Collins Press
West Link Park
Doughcloyne
Wilton
Cork

British Library Cataloguing in Publication Data
Horgan, Joseph.
The song at your backdoor.
1. Horgan, Joseph–Homes and haunts–Ireland–Cork
(County) 2. Natural history–Ireland–Cork (County)
3. Natural history in literature. 4. Cork (Ireland :
County)–Rural conditions. 5. Ireland–In literature.
I. Title
508.4'195-dc22
ISBN-13: 9781848890336

Typesetting by The Collins Press
Typeset in AGaramond
Printed in Great Britain by CPI Cox & Wyman

Cover images
Birds © iStockphoto/Nicholas; Tree © iStockphoto/Ace_Create

Contents

Always for Kitty
You've been a friend to me

Oh come you back my own true love
Come you back and stay a while with me
If ever I had a friend on earth
You've been a friend to me
So fare you well my own true love
And fare you well for a while
I'm going away but I'll be back
If I go ten thousand miles

Traditional Song

All great civilisations are based on parochialism. To know fully even one field or one land is a lifetime's experience. In the world of poetic experience it is depth that counts, not width. A gap in a hedge, a smooth rock surfacing a narrow lane, a view of a woody meadow, the stream at the junction of four small fields, these are as much as a man can fully experience.[1]

Patrick Kavanagh

Introduction

I t begins with the swallows. I came out of the backdoor and heard them and looked up and saw them. I tried to follow their patterns. Tried to trace them. Patrick Kavanagh's assertion about a field or a land led me on.

This book is a walk, by and large, criss-crossing over eight or nine miles of land. It is about a yard and a lane, though it does take in those land edges and roads a further distance away. I did not believe that I would get to know this stretch of land fully. This book does not pretend to be that. As Kavanagh states, that is a lifetime's experience. I did stop, nonetheless, at the gap in a hedge, at the rock on a lane, at the view to a wood, at a stream in a field. I wanted to see.

Writing in the 1940s, the Irish botanist Robert Lloyd Praeger talked of 'the mind jaded with the meaningless noise and hurry of modern life'.[2] In the 1940s. I have tried not to start off from that point. Some rubbing against, some friction with modern society, has been inevitable in a book delving into the natural world but I have not set off from there. I have not journeyed away from something but have tried instead to move towards, to get to. I wanted the experience that Patrick Kavanagh intimated was in the land, wanted to find it, wanted to arrive at a clearer understanding of place and of a place in the world. A place on earth. I walked the lanes and had a look around.

I have attempted to make the book an organic thing and have wanted as far as possible for it to grow in a way that was dictated by the fields, by the land. By the swallows. I did not, of course, succeed in that. Writing is an artificial act. A book is a built construct. I had to put a structure in place. I had to manufacture and assemble it. I had to author it. Even so, the lanes walked and the things seen did dictate the pages. The otters and the seals, the ravens and peregrines, the jackdaws and the starlings. I did not order them.

And one fundamental characteristic of these pages is not really one that was initially in my mind at all. I did not set out thinking it would play such a part. The lanes, though, the weather and the birds, they led me to it. I had not realised that other books would come into this book so much. I did not think that culture would walk here with nature and in that I could not have been more wrong. Everywhere I went there was the company of someone who had gone before me, somebody pointing the way, pointing something out. I was led towards other books. When I got there I pinched and stole and nicked. I make no apology for that. Not only were their words and their insights better than mine, but that is what I set out for. I wanted to know, wanted to find out. I wanted a clearer understanding. So I used books. Any misinterpretations that occur are solely my fault, any enlightenments are theirs. Those books, by the time of my arrival, were part of the fields and the lanes too. I suspect that is what Kavanagh meant all along.

One other characteristic of this work I will own up to. This book sets out to celebrate the ordinary. When I stood in the concrete of this old yard and heard the blackbird sing, I knew that was what I wanted to do. I wanted to seek in the forgotten corners, the old fields, the rough country. I wanted to record the starling beneath the leaking corrugated roof and the sparrow in the crumbling wooden board. Sure, the otter and the seal, the peregrine falcon are here too, but I did not choose them because of their ratings value. I found them. I went over the cliffs and the rocks, alongside the lagoons and the forest, revelling in their beauty. But their beauty can speak loudly for itself. This book always comes back to the yard.

In *The Song of the Earth*, one of the books I found along the way, one that found its way again and again into this book, Jonathan Bate writes of attempting to live with a 'thoughtfulness and with an attentiveness, an attunement to both words and the world, and so to acknowledge that although we make sense of things by way of words, we do not live apart from the world'.[3] I did not realise how large a part words, culture, the writings of others would play, when I opened the backdoor to have a look around. I was truly mistaken.

I always returned to the earth itself though. Nature was always the first call, the first contact. It always began there. There were many, many words waiting to be found along the way but the world itself was always the beginning. I knew that much at least, always knew how it would begin.

It begins with the swallows.

Today's core belief is that nature is in the past.[1]

Richard Louv

1

The Middle State

The bypass, as much a salient feature of the average Irish town now as the convent used to be, steels its way past the mudflats of the bay, the row of bright houses, the courthouse, the small shops and the auctioneers, the old school, the new playground, and curves back again to join the road heading west. It goes by one of the few remaining fields within the town boundary. It goes by the old show grounds where the annual agricultural show is still held and where piebald horses graze beside industrial units. At certain times of day this bypass is busy. In the morning and evening. At school pick-up time. Cars flow on and on. Cars go east and cars go west. Where it joins the road again, the old road that goes straight through the town, there is a new supermarket. It is part of a national chain that brings its own identity with it, an identity proudly independent of its surroundings; a little corner of everywhere.

Turn off the bypass before reaching this and on the right there is a widened road. The road has only recently been extended and there is still a grey patina of dust in the air. It has been widened because, beyond a short straggle of older houses, a new estate has been built. The estate is fronted by a grey, imposing wall and is gated. New houses, avenues of domesticity and suburban living, drift away beyond sight. There is a name set in the stone entrance that, as I pass, I don't catch. A new address. I remember once, not far from here, an old woman telling someone, who was describing their new house, what the name of the field it stood in had been. And the names of the fields around it. And the fields beyond that. Remembering only the roll of green and the lines of ditch she was able to list off a lot of names.

Now that roll call of names could be seen as merely a straying into memory, as a collection of curious nomenclature, as part of a random foray into the past. Or it could be seen very differently. That litany of place names could be seen as the equivalent of a map. In that case the names of those fields would not be a simple procession of random labels but words that tell us something intrinsic about the land, part of what has been called a 'venerable, if patchy, folk natural history.'[2] Those names would then be something lending the fields an identity, giving the landscape a ready essence. Those names would make it easy to see how through 'places, place lore, placenames: the landscape of Ireland was seen and read by the Irish through powerful cultural lenses.'[3] Of course, with the fields now having a new name, there would seem to be a new way of reading them, a new cultural prism. This has, though, all happened before. The Irish landscape has been re-imagined many times. From the first farmers who began to clear and make fields to the Elizabethan settlers who, even as Spenser was seeing the place as one 'Of woods and forests, which therein abound/ Sprinkled with wholsom waters',[4] were setting about removing the remaining forests. Or the Ordnance Survey cartographers who came and mapped the country, with different names in a different language; 'mapping the place and thinking up new names for it'[5] as Brian Friel so simply puts it. In fact, it has always been the case that the altering of the landscape, which has often been in effect the clearing of the landscape, has been a psychological one as much as a physical one and that this has involved viewing what was already there as inherently worthless and outdated. The aboriginal countryside always had to be emptied of mental lumber as much as any other kind. So such things as placenames are easily discarded and considered as having no intrinsic worth. Part, primarily of an oral tradition, that is essentially invisible and always off the page, they can disappear easily. History, whether natural or social, has accorded what it has often dismissed as mere folklore very little attention and such is the hiatus between the oral tradition and the written record that there is often the act of recording only as something is vanishing, with the richness and in many ways the accuracy of this tradition then lost. Admittedly, this is a historical source that is often broken and fragmentary, 'venerable, if patchy', and in some regards strongly limited by being so tied to locality. Yet, this should not be allowed to undervalue it. It can still form an essential part of what Cathal Póirtéir has called 'the mosaic of our understanding'.[6] Every road, field and stream in the country, it is often said, had a name and in a once deeply rural, densely populated country that is not hard to imagine. After all, there are across the country some 60,000 townland names alone. The cartographer and writer Tim Robinson has written eloquently about this very aspect of the Irish landscape: 'In countless place names the web of stone has caught something of the words of those generations who were so hard pressed that all their toil left them possessing nothing, scarcely a musical instrument, a cart for seaweed or a boat to fish the teeming sea, nothing but the immaterial arts they were so rich in.'[7]

A good part of those immaterial arts was, of course, that of language, of talk, of naming. In the name of a field there is not merely a title deed but a story, a background, an aside about the country, a country that was not mapped in any kind of recorded, substantial way, as apart from the purely imaginative kind, until sometime after the 1520s; quite late by European standards. The mental mapping of Ireland was replaced by the military, the economic, the colonial. It is now, in ways that are not at first obvious, being substantially mapped again. The landscape has been re-imagined and renamed once more and with each new address an old address is forgotten, with each new name an older name is lost.

Not so long ago I was coming through this same place as dark was falling and I saw the glare of car lights stationary up ahead. I thought I could hear children screaming. As I passed the field I realised that what I saw and heard was the hunting of rabbits and the running of dogs. It was the kind of casually brutal scene it is still easy to find in the countryside. The people standing by the cars felt no sentimentality about the hundreds of white-tailed rabbits running around the ploughed ground, or about the ploughed ground itself. Maybe, they already thought, this field will soon be full of earth-moving machinery anyway. The poet John Montague has written of this: that what characterises so much of the Irish landscape now is not farming, but demolition. 'Watch the giant machines trundle over/This craggy land, crushing old contours,/Trampling down the nearly naked earth.'[8] The geographer Patrick Duffy touched upon similar themes when he described much recent development as being akin to 'a form of landscape trauma'.[9] Observing the new estate now and the pile of moved earth beside it, like a sudden hill, it is sobering to realise that much of what has been fundamentally reshaped here is land that gained its essential shape over 13,000 years ago. The land I look at had held that now vanished form since the ice sheets finally retreated. Since then, along those thousands and thousands of years, nothing else had come along to alter that scoured outline. Nothing until now. Its surface had changed beyond recognition, yes, forest had come and gone amid drastic alteration to the Irish environment but the fundamental ground pattern had remained. Until now this shape, this outline, had largely continued intact. Such, indeed, has been the history of this country and the comparatively limited effect of man upon it, that a 'pristine and primeval'[10] landscape is thought to have survived here well into modern historical times, with some even suggesting into the 1970s that 'Ireland retains landscapes which have all but disappeared in Britain.'[11] In this way, with a different history of human activity, an undeveloped economy and a different pattern of social settlement, in some way the 'natural', elusive as that is, survived here in Ireland for much longer than it did elsewhere, in particular in comparison to our nearest ecological and geographical neighbour. Now some of that may well be contestable, but there is no doubt that having missed out on the industrial revolution, rural life and social patterns, and therefore landscapes, were less intrinsically altered here than they were elsewhere. Even, it has been visibly clear, to the extent that the physical appearance of Ireland once the wood had gone, leaving only the soil and the rock behind, remained little changed. Indeed, because that very wood had gone, much of the built environment, that once housed a pre-Famine population still well in excess of what we have now, vanished, fell away back into the earth it was made from and left the land relatively untouched. For centuries the basic topography of the country was generally unaltered. Of course, fields were enlarged and towns sometimes grew and more solid buildings appeared but only recently, minutely recently in geological terms, did the very shape of the land begin to be altered to any great extent, in any kind of elemental way. The post-glacial shape, the skin of the Irish landscape, the surface that might have appeared as the final ordering, is only now being peeled away. I do not know what name, if any, there was for that particular field, the field where dogs caught rabbits and where house lights now shine. I do know it has a name now though, now that it is, in effect, gone.

Back on the bypass the traffic goes on. Sometimes it halts at a crossing and a person makes their way across. Sometimes it breaks to let some new car join the stream and there is a wave and an acknowledgement. Children play in a bright playground beside it, the tall goals of a pitch behind them. Just outside the town, from time to time, council workers in bright yellow jackets and clipboards stand beside the road. Talking to them on one occasion they told me that they were doing a traffic count. They counted, they said, the thousands and thousands of cars that passed backwards and forwards every day. Sometime, they supposed, these numbers would determine the future of the road. Not so long ago, someone had told me, before the bypass was built, the family dog used to lie out just off this road. Children grew up and barely a car passed. It is even true that within living memory rural Ireland could have been said to be more or less car free. Now it is not unusual to see four or five cars outside an average house and on dark evenings the road is a stream of moving headlights. At times it is as if the old core of the town has itself been bypassed. The old pubs and the old shops that are increasingly refitted so that they take on the character of pubs and shops anywhere. The main road becoming indistinct with chain stores and franchises. Down one small side street, into a quiet corner, a small pub leans against a much taller building that was once a warehouse. Somebody told me that as a child going to school in the town, only thirty odd years ago, she saw a barn owl flying out of that building nearly every winter evening. It is now renovated and reoccupied and the barn owl is gone. In between winter cars now a jackdaw drops down to a bin or the locally called 'lady wagtail' walks delicately along the kerb.

Turn off the bypass again and go back up the widened road that leads to the gated estate. Note the ditches still white with dust. See the blackberries, a little off being ready to pick, the tough, aggressive, native bush, thriving and coming back even after being scrubbed; the insistent, straggly, messy, wild fruit known to everyone; the 'little humped one'[12] that mad Sweeney complained of tearing him. Such, indeed, is the strength of this plant's link with us and our ancestors that it has been recorded in the stomach of Neolithic man. It is hardly surprising though that he would have sought out the bite of its purple berries. As the summer closed he would have seen the large clusters of fruit at the end of the old shoots, searched out the fullest one, the lowest one that sits right at the tip of the stalk. Soon the smaller berries further up the stalk would ripen but it would be nearly October then and they would be hard and bitter. Back in the town now, cultivated brambles are for sale, tamed and suitable for the garden. It used to be that it was only the blackberry's sister plant, the raspberry, that was taken in, planted beside the lawn or the rows of vegetables. Now, the cultivated plant of the thorny bramble may well adorn the patches of grass in the new estate, growing where the wild variety, until very recently, still pushed through. Similarly, in the supermarket just below here, the fruits of the blackberry are for sale in plastic punnets that were filled not from these lanes a few hundred yards away but in the fields of another country.

Where the original wild bramble still clings on beside the road we can halt for a moment. Beyond the ditch a large field of tall corn spreads away, a slight hint of yellow inside the waving green. There is stillness in the closing day, merely the slight shifting of a breeze. Just here, still within reach of the busy bypass and the passing cars, within the evening glare of the supermarket lights and in sight of the new estate, there is a peculiar, eye-catching scene. The sky is raining hundreds and hundreds of small birds. They fall, oblivious to the human endeavour around them. They rise again unaware, unconcerned. Above the entire field they proceed. They are their own world. They are a shower of silent swallows.

They are not silent in a complete way but silent compared with their midsummer screaming, when they chase each other endlessly, breathlessly around the yard. Silent in comparison to the screeching that accompanies their diving through the sky in displays that, while there may be no biological evidence to support this, appear like nothing but exhibitions of joy. Silent compared with the nestling whistles that greet their entering of barns at speeds that seem impossible, until a last invisible swerve brings the flash of a feeding bird through a small gap.

There is none of that now above the cornfield. In the still air the birds move silently as if tracing smoke. Their flight is languid and without haste. From time to time a high-pitched noise escapes and drifts down but it carries none of the intensity or urgency of those summer voices. The overarching silence has a strange, indefinable quality and it spreads as I watch. No one would have to strain to hear it. No one would have to concentrate. It leaves the noises of the town behind and the small interruptions from one or other bird are simply a lacuna to its completeness. Swallows, impossible to count, dance above the corn in a display of silent movement. The continual motion, the flying in and out, up and down, the irregular high-pitched note, this is what it creates. Something other.

It is late now in the summer, that time when the season is only clinging on and autumn brings chill to the morning, to the evening and the shade. This is, in all likelihood, a mass gathering that is a precursor to migration. The swallow is, of course, one of our great examples of bird migration and in many ways the most wondrous as it is the one we can see from our kitchen windows and our front doors. Its very familiarity belies the fantastic nature of its existence; the journey it undertakes from here to southern Africa and from there, some five months later, back here to Ireland. It is with us from April onwards; the birds who return to our sheds having arrived on the twelfth of April for the last three years. Not only do they return but they return, faithful year after faithful year, to the same nest sites, sites that are now usually associated with human habitation. We can forgive ourselves for imagining that their fidelity is something of an attachment to us. Once they nested in the chimney shafts of houses but it is now outhouses and stables, where the joists and corners can support the mud bowl that is the nest. The forsaking of older ancestral sites, though, on sea cliff and cave may now be seen as unwise for it may be that swallow numbers are declining. It might appear unlikely to think in these terms whilst watching such a multitude of the species and having observed them all summer long but there are easy, sobering examples to hand of how the common can become the rare. I have two bird guides here, both from the early 1980s. Both confidently list the corncrake, another summer visitor from as far away as the African continent, as present over all of Ireland and as 'common throughout the west and southwest'.[13] As late as 1972 there were still parts of the island where there were said to be a pair of birds per acre. Not afraid or particularly shy of man, though there was some evidence to suggest that it showed itself 'decidedly more freely'[14] in Ireland than it did in Britain, even into the 1960s it was reported nesting in industrial Dublin and the suburbs of Belfast. It was not often seen, apart from, perhaps, the neck that would crane above the long grass, but it was often heard. Yet, the incessant night-time call said to be so characteristic of this bird is now nothing but a memory, even here in the southwest, where it was once so ubiquitous. That bird sound has gone and silence has arrived within the space of a mere twenty-odd years. This would have been hard to picture back then, when every field would have seemed to house a corncrake but it has happened now and whilst the bird lingers on in certain parts of this country the 'catastrophic decline' that the guidebooks tell of is almost certainly irreversible. All of this with a species of bird once so common that it was said 'corncrakes in the meadows on a summer day were part of the unchanging order of things'.[15] The unchanging order of things.

It is now being suggested, as global warming takes effect, that more and more swallows are only migrating as far as the southern tip of Spain and whilst the bird is yet plentiful and its numbers merely being monitored the concern is that this might be indicative of significant change. It is also being suggested, much like the early and mechanised mowing of fields was said to have decimated the corncrake, that farmyards cleansed of flies and generally sanitised, along with outhouses converted into human use are all elements slowly contributing to a fall in swallow numbers. Of course, our migratory birds are always susceptible to factors far away from here: the vast netting of corncrakes along migratory routes must have impacted as much upon numbers as farming changes did. The fall in swallow numbers too is likely to involve any number of extraneous factors but in terms of those farmyards and outhouses we are referring to the decline, in effect, of Irish agriculture. The ornithologist Tony Soper wrote that on restoring a derelict outhouse, something that has now taken place across Ireland, the saddest part was seeing a swallow return to its now blocked-off nest site. 'For several days it continually flew up to the window and sought vainly for a way in. I remember very well how keenly it demonstrated its longing.'[16] Longing, we could say, would have to be part of a bird that exists the way this does, even if that longing is only the chemistry of cells.

In our sophistication we have relegated the arrival of the swallow to the slightly sardonic letter in a newspaper. It is unlikely that this was always so and there are records of rural traditions where the arrival was greeted with a less mannered leap in the air. Indeed there was a time not so long ago when the swallow's life pattern was even more incredible than it is now. It was believed for centuries, here and elsewhere, that swallows spent the winter beneath damp mud, primarily the mud of estuaries. As David Cabot recounts, 'the large pre-migratory flocks congregating in the autumn, their wheeling over reed beds, their subsequent disappearance and mysterious re-emergence the following spring led many naturalists to believe that at some stage they buried themselves in the soft ooze'.[17] Of course, this made sense. When the other side of the world was as far-fetched as the idea that these small birds might go there, it was clear that, once they reached the coast, it was there they vanished, into the soft, bottomless mud beside the sea. In that way, in those years, they never actually left us, they did not cross unimaginable oceans, they simply drifted off into a different existence. Giraldus Cambrensis, in his study of Ireland, the *Topographia Hiberniae* of 1188, informs us of those 'birds that do not appear in the winter time', that they are in fact 'seized up into a long ecstasy and some middle state between life and death'.[18] Swallows did not go to faraway lands over faraway seas. They did not physically depart. That was simply unbelievable. They did disappear though. They did become invisible. They went to a 'middle state between life and death'.

Centuries later the flock above the cornfield is surely gathering at the behest of some call within, something deep within their small frames. Some bloodstream bell of migration. Some tissue, some gland that is now responding to the shortening daylight. Something within, calling them to begin a round journey of over 10,000 miles. It is said that good weather is often a precursor to migration, that the high atmospheric pressure, the anticyclonic conditions, will lure the birds into the sky. They will fly out to those estuary muds and, stretching belief even though we know it to be true, carry on to the southern tip of another continent where they will herald summer there as much as they do here. The swallows will travel across those miles during daylight, unlike the other small, migratory, insectivorous birds, that seek the cover of night, and they will take sustenance en route. Yard-reared birds will fly over mountains, oceans, deserts and the tropics. Yet in the evening air, metres away from the insistent bypass and the sudden supermarket, it is the near-silent movement of these same birds that defeats me. I stand beneath and beside their silent dance and for this nonscientific moment, these pre-enlightenment seconds, I feel close to that 'ancient assumption, of an intimate traffic between human beings and nature'.[19] I feel drawn into a thinking that once was. My mind struggles to fully comprehend this. My imagination is unable to contain it. The flight and the stillness. The ease of movement, as if they proceeded, this confetti of birds, above the plain corn, within a different atmosphere. A stillness that the eye cannot retain. As if molecules and atoms, chemistry and physics, sound and sight, were following different rules here. As if for this moment they are in a state beyond me. Even, perhaps, as if they are nearing some middle state, some state between life and death. The middle state. Is this what it would look like?

In summer I lift the children to nests in the sheds. Squat, blue-black bodies, thin yellow lines of a beak, squeeze themselves into the beaded mud bowls high on the beams above us, these simple circles of local architecture. As I lean one child forward, a wooden inner gate cracks beneath me and throughout the winter I can see that tear in the wood, the white scar slowly darkening. There is a creak there now that does not go away. On a grey day in December, simply passing through, it will remind me of summer. When those swallows have ventured from the nest, lining up on wires within the shed, they still let us approach. I'm not sure if these are the same screeching birds who career around the yard chasing their parents' graceful irregularity or whether this approachability only exists before the ability of flight but for now we can stand within touching distance of their bodies. When it is late in the summer and these birds are of the second or third brood this proximity is just a few weeks away from the moment when they will haul their tiny frames to another continent. Incubated for about two weeks and ready to fly at the grand age of twenty-one days, these later birds, these broods of four or five chicks, face daunting odds. Within the same time frame again they must prepare to leave. Many, many, many will die. Small bodies will drop exhaustedly into ocean or valley or field or street. They will have known only this small yard and far away from the middle state they will have failed.

I take the bypass again and now the year has definitely turned. The last few nights have seen a huge moon resting over the fields, a clear sky, midnight light you could read by, and the first hint of real cold. In these early days of October I still see far above the sheds a swallow or two flying by. They still tread their joyous patterns. When there was a spell of bad, lowering weather a few days back it seemed as if they had gone. There was none of their darting colour in the grey sky and it appeared as if summer's collapse had buried them. It is thought that the odd, solitary individual, the outlying bird of a social species, does stay and swallows have been recorded into January and February. Whether this is faulty biological wiring or wilfulness, who can tell? Science in all its beauty falters somewhat when it comes to the exception. But exceptions there are. The swallow that appears above a building in December. The flight of tail feathers months before they are expected. Movements in the air that reach beyond our understanding, that when recorded do not fit into our records, that exist beyond our bureaucratic minds. Epistemology, as the philosophers call it, tested by a stray bird.

Whereas the solitary, staying swallow is often just a rumour, we have some definite examples of a natural peculiarity with our hooded crows. I would have passed some on the way here, perhaps on the soccer pitch in the show grounds. Amongst the uniform blackness of most other crows their grey-shawled shoulders stand out, a strangely medieval, ecclesiastical appearance. The hooded crow is usually categorised as a subspecies of the carrion crow and the two races are said to have become separated during one of the ice ages. Here in the southwest corner of Ireland they are a common sight, yet a short flight over the Irish Sea they are only present in the northern stretch of Britain, in a territory further north than anything on this island. As a subspecies of the carrion crow they are said to be found as a northern and eastern counterpart to it. Yet, here they are in Ireland as a southern and western presence. A crow of 'different colours' as Giraldus puts it when noting their presence and the black crows' absence. In this way they break what naturalists call 'conventional distribution patterns', where the presence of the birds here should mirror the presence of the birds on our neighbouring island. It does not. Life knows nothing of our categories, however particularly, even lovingly, they are constructed. A strange swallow lingers, the hooded crow is common far further south than its neighbours. We draw up categories and straight-lined accounts and try to squeeze everything in, but a rogue wing feather and the careful page is a mess.

A few days later I turn off again before the bypass coils around and take the widened road. The bramble is now carrying the smaller berries that appear higher up the stalk but there is still, despite the lateness of the year, the occasional fat berry to be eaten, to be picked. By the bramble and opposite the cornfield I stop. There is a soft rise in the field above me and the crop moves in the breeze. I can hear the continuous, low, interference of the road. The heavy swing of two unloved rooks passes by overhead and I glance up. Apart from the lumbering black shapes the sky is empty. The sky is empty. There are no swallows. I have misjudged. There is no gathering. They have moved on. Perhaps they are flying over the sea even now, their slender bodies, their long wings and their trailing forked tails. The younger ones, this year's brood without the length of streaming tail, taking their maiden voyage. The last ones, the late summer crop, up there too, survival odds stacked against them. But some of these, even some of these weeks-old birds, do make it. Some of these get to go and come back. Though most, it must be admitted, do not. Suddenly their effortless flight around the safety of the yard, all that easy power, seems very like the child's play it so resembled. There is nothing now disturbing the air above the corn. No oriental hint of miniature stillness. No state but the one that can be easily seen.

There is a place that I have gone to since childhood that is not too far from here. It is only a few miles from this spot. When I get there I can sit on a headland that overlooks the sea and perhaps yet see some departing birds. More than likely, though, it will be spring and cold, bright days, before I see them again. Seduced by the middle state, I will have missed their farewell.

The landscape is a most important fact in our lives. We live in it and move around in it, it is the daily context of our experience as human beings.[1]

Patrick Duffy

2

Desire Paths

Town planners have a phrase for the shortcuts people in the city choose to take instead of the designed ones the planner has created. These worn routes, though they often appear rough and sad, the bare grass leading down from the high-rise flats, the road-crossing that avoids the subway, the gap over the fence, the cut through the back of the garages, all of these are called 'desire paths'. I am not sure whether this is supposed to be a term of disapproval or a term that is meant to celebrate the expression of human life. Whatever the case, it does denote how people respond in unexpected ways to an environment over which they have little or no control, an environment that in an urban setting can often seem to exist only as a passing blur from a car window. They create routes where none were supposed to be. They follow some other impulse above that of the lines on the architect's map. They find themselves unable to live inside the technical drawing. In some indefinable way this is always heartening. The walk across the open space that ignores the concrete path installed by the planners may not be much but even as a sliver of the imagination it is something.

Like the city the country is veined with desire paths. Roads follow no discernible route, meandering at will, as if led by a curious eye. Before organic became a buzzword of a certain commercial bent it was present here in the very formation of the landscape. It was how roads appeared or fields were hedged, wearing themselves into the earth in accordance with the natural topography, rather than simply imposing themselves as modern roads so often do. It was a time when, as Vidal de la Blanche puts it, a landscape 'resembled a medal struck in the likeness of a people'.[2] Maybe, with our fading bungalows and our grand, gated homes, it still does. But, while the straight eye and square box of the suburb has certainly appeared now in the Irish countryside, that severity has yet to overwhelm the ragged line of the fields or the unending inconsistency of a road. That is not to say that a directness of eye and route is unknown here. I write this at the top of a boreen and at the bottom of it there is a road that runs straight through to the next village. It dips slightly from time to time and though the uneven country alongside it does not offer a clearness of perspective the road itself stretches out straight ahead. It is the kind of road that makes journeying itself a simple pleasure. It is not a road, for all its unswerving intent, that is meant for passing. It is a road that is meant for halting. No one who walked it would ever have done so without stopping or would have travelled it at great speed. It is not built like that.

Yet, perhaps, that is where I err. Straight roads probably always carried an air of efficiency about them. What I am probably guilty of is lending those qualities the road now possesses a shine they would not originally have had. When every road was quiet or virtually free of cars, when every road could be journeyed by human beings rather than vehicles, this road would have been unremarkable. It is only now, when even in the countryside a peaceful thoroughfare is rare, that it has taken on the context it has. Aside from the few moments of a hurried, speeding car, most of the day on this road reaches quietly off into the distance.

Apart from the rooks and jackdaws noisily roosting along it or the GAA pitch sometimes drawing a crowd it is a road above which the western sky restlessly shifts and where the silence of an unmechanical moment can still be found. It is a road to stop on, climb out on, and listen on. A road to stand still on, to be still on. It does not appear to have changed over the decades and remains a road where it is easy to imagine, just for instance, as the loneliness of a fading summer evening closes in, streams of 1950s' emigrants departing, suitcases in hand, family waved away. They stride off for the passing Cork bus a few miles further on and suitably enough they do so along a straight road that could have been designed by the planners of the future. Walking off to the future they carry either their broken hearts or their fresh breaths of freedom, or more likely, both. The novelist John Banville remembered them decades later:

> There they were, the crowds of awkward, lost young men with their cardboard suitcases, heading for the building sites of places with cruel-sounding names: Hackney, Wolverhampton, Liverpool, the Bronx. Many years later, at the very end of the 1960s when I was living in London, I would see them again, these same men, grown older and harder but still awkward, still lost, playing mournful two-man games of hurling in Hyde Park on summer Sunday mornings.[3]

Travelling the road in late September I see a swallow, continually leaving and arriving, darting low over a field, a bird that could not twist itself into a straightness of flight if it were to spend the whole summer trying.

Considering the often tortured history between this island and the island that was the destination of most of those emigrants it always seems symbolic that within a study of the natural world Ireland's truest ecological context is alongside that of Britain.[4] So I always find it interesting to note that the swallows that visit our shores and the swallows that visit those of our neighbouring island often winter in different countries in southern Africa. They come, in a way, from different parts of the world. These differences within an ecological context though, come even more forcibly to mind when I walk the path that eventually leads to the headland by the sea, the headland where I hope to see the last of those departing swallows and see, instead, the choughs.

The way to the headland begins some five or six miles outside town and is at the end of the old road to the sea. There is a view of the ocean on a rise in this road and you can often see water breaking against the rocks that sit in the middle of the bay whilst still a long way from the shore. The green arms of the land can be seen, the blues of sea and sky, the living, moving white of the breaking waves. On a jut of land to the right there is a lighthouse and the curve of that coast gives this little stretch of strand its protection. There are often reports now of whales being seen off the rocks there and a whole industry of Irish whale-spotting has grown up. Incredibly, the second biggest animal to have ever existed, the fin whale, can be found just here off the Irish coast. Farmers on the land that slips down to these cliffs will happily tell you that they have always seen these huge mammals breaking the water, whatever new world the whale recorders think they have discovered, bringing home to us how the recording of nature has been as much about the observer as the observed. The sea then disappears from view as the undulating road dips down and on a small road off to the left the way to the headland continues. Very quickly this road enters a small gathering of bungalows and tidy cottages.

In many ways this gathering, this flurry of housing, represents an earlier pattern of Irish settlement than that of the individual farmhouse we are so familiar with. Pre-Famine Ireland, unlike the de-peopled, silent country that came after, was said to be 'densely populated, unruly, dangerous but energetic'[5] and contained an Irish landscape that would have been characterised by 'small cabin clusters located within the network of townlands'.[6] That very much sums up the character of the settlement I see before me. Back home, too, I have an old survey map of the farmhouse where I will write this all up that dates from, as far as I can ascertain, August 1845. That farmhouse sits at the end of a long approach lane and apart from three outbuildings is now surrounded only by sycamore trees and old hedging. On the old map though, in this same spot, some twelve buildings are marked. The old pattern suggests that there would have been a good number of people residing there, perhaps in the humble cabins mentioned before, the kind of homes that would leave little obvious trace. The parish record for the wider townland also tells something of this story. It reveals that in 1841 the population was 227 souls, which does suggest a gathering of such buildings, to house such a density of people. It also reveals what came after though, in that by 1851 this population had shrunk to just 79.

Strangely enough, the current cluster of buildings I pass through also carries with it a sense of another feature of the built Irish environment: that of the deserted and abandoned homesteads that until so recently marked the rural scene. Clearly most of these houses are holiday homes and this late in September their migrant owners have returned to their first homes. Amongst such a number of houses, past such well-maintained lawns, the stillness and quietness is somewhat disconcerting, as if mirroring the empty places of thirty and forty years ago. Or perhaps, mirroring even more, the empty commuter estates and houses of today, for in a very revealing reflection of our age, this area here contains many of the most recent developments of Irish society. Only thirty-odd years ago this was a completely rural set of townlands, a place that was only a few fields away from the harsh swell of the Atlantic. Yes, there were holidaymakers here but the post-office-cum-pub served primarily farmers and there was still the chance of hearing Irish spoken. Now it is one of the most select areas surrounding the town and at the beginning of the day a place that is marked by a line of large cars making their way back towards the town and from there up to the city. It is a place where commuters live and where their ever-larger houses now dominate. A place where the 'landscape amnesia' that seems to have gripped so much of the country is evident, where the link with the previous remembered environment does not, in any obvious way, exist.[7] A place, like so many others, where Ireland seems to have begun again from scratch.

A short way beyond the holiday homes there is an old farmhouse where a shy dog sometimes hides and a smiling farmer always waves. Here is one of the many examples of that other Ireland, the one we have already spoken of, where the 'dominance of proudly independent scattered farms and the weakness of long-established village communities',[8] symbolises the Irish rural scene. It is as if these Irelands are nestling side by side. Very quickly the pathway now becomes an uneven boreen with a long track of grass growing down the middle. Here the road begins to rise again and the huge eyes of healthy black-and-white cows watch. The sea is still hidden from view but there is often a taste of it in the air. A vast bull stands in the middle of a field ignoring passers-by with the indifference of sheer strength. The path is now dirt and grass, though beyond the gate the grassy path has been newly laid with gravel and there is a creeping tidiness. In a little hollow off to the right there is a grotto and a statue of the Virgin Mary, in enduring blue and white, looks out to where the sea sounds behind the rocks. There is an altar in this lovingly maintained spot, where an August Mass is said once a year and I wonder was it once the site of a Mass rock, or whether it is the well that gives up such cold, refreshing water that has drawn worshippers here. Sadly ignorant, though I have been here countless times and attended the Mass here many times as a boy, I take a drink of water and let the coolness fill my throat. It is likely that this crystal-clear water, springing fresh from the earth, means this spot was held in veneration even before the coming of Christianity, becoming a holy well as time went on. The ice-cold water sings in my mouth. I sit awhile and think, as others must have done before me.

Just beyond the grotto the ground becomes very broken and the path nearly vanishes amongst encroaching heather and unseen potholes. Beneath the low cover there is the sound of water and the snaking evidence of a stream making its way to the sea. Through the side of the cliff, a little further on, this stream leaves the rock and water plummets continuously into the ocean. A few years ago, in Mayo, I recall we came across lazy beds whose ridged lines went right down to the edge of the land. Here, though, the dark heaviness of rock is never far away and soil is at such a premium that even lazy beds would seem impossible. Yet, soon, there is a relieving patch of rush and the bite of the aggressive heather spikes is forgotten. The vegetation here is tough, hardy, resistant, surviving on the edge of the island, where land ends and sea begins. Walking through here once I flushed a hare whose relative hugeness belied an incredible speed. In a blur of disturbed undergrowth it was gone. What is particularly interesting about the hare, though, is that here too is an Irish species that is something of a zoological discrepancy. The Irish hare is considered a distinct subspecies of the mountain hare, mainly because the Irish hare does not turn white in summer, but even more notably the distribution of the mountain hare in Ireland is thought of as being 'most unusual',[9] and again our neighbouring island might offer the best example of why. In Britain the mountain hare is mostly confined to the upland moors of Scotland with the brown hare being the species found in England and Wales. Here, by contrast, the brown hare is only found as an introduced species, with a now uncertain status, whilst the northern mountain hare is found throughout the island from mountaintop to sea level, from the northern coast to the southern tip I stand on. So this species, one of Ireland's longest established creatures, one of the earliest colonists, also contravenes the accepted patterns of species distribution. The Irish hare breaks the rules. It has actually been dated here to before the last ice sheets, though we cannot be sure it survived the subsequent return of the cold, or simply came back again. For such a long established species it is sobering to think that these blurs of speed have such a high mortality rate. As many as 80 per cent die in their first year and an average of about 50 per cent die each year. Those who reach the maximum eight or nine years must be remarkable creatures indeed.

Just here the ocean can be heard, the sucking, clapping and banging, the percussion it beats against the rock. Suddenly, there is a sense of wilderness, of a habitat where man is an infrequent visitor. A mere few minutes in and the land runs out and cliffs fall off into the sea. I lean carefully against a bank of earth on the other side of which there is a drop to the water below. Here there is a small, sheltered inlet, accessible only by boat. The water is clear and deep and on this day there is only a little whitening from the swell. Some wrack floats just beneath the surface and I can see and hear now where the stream breaks through and a waterfall tumbles into the sea. Some rock doves suddenly take flight and they veer along past the outcrops of cliff. These purely wild doves, the ancestors of all those city pigeons and domestic racers, nest along these sheer cliffs, raising a brood in the unlikely gap of a crevice. Unlike their impoverished, straggly, urban descendants these birds are fast and sleek. Often on a city street I have seen the much maligned city pigeon looking thin and bedraggled, sometimes carrying a deformed or missing foot. These cliff-side birds are nothing like that. Still living in their ancient evolutionary niche they, though not numerous, are strong-looking birds. I have heard it said that between the cliff-side and the waves of the sea, the high-rise building and the traffic of the streets, the environment of the two sets of birds may not be as different as at first seems. The purer rock doves, though, have none of their city cousins' approachability and these shyer cliff dwellers spin off around the rocks at high speed and are gone. I turn to watch them go and seeing the sea widen out before me and the coastline spread off into the distance I find the comparison between the two environments a stretch too far, whatever the acceptance that the doves do not reside here for aesthetic reasons.

On a rock below where I stand, on a finger of cliff that juts out to the sea, a group of cold-eyed herring gulls sit. A lone cormorant sits amongst them, drying its open wings. They are all looking out to sea, all sitting facing the same direction, as if waiting. They do not seem willing to be disturbed by my presence and have none of the rapid shyness of the doves. I sit above them for a while and look out to sea too.

The path along soon becomes very narrow. Here the fields end and as I pass beyond the heather-strewn rock patches there are indeed fields that go right up to the land's edge. There is evidence of man's activities, here where the sea begins, in the remnants of stone walls that have fallen away and which now divide field from nothing more than air. On my right the cliff falls away and a step to the side is a drop on to rock or ocean. The unceasing green and blue, the white, of the sea. I am suddenly, acutely aware that the only thing that might not be competent traversing this place, might not be equipped to survive it for even a short while, is me. The land finishes unevenly and the contours of the cliff curve in and out like an imprint of the beating sea. A little way along and there is a sudden hole in the ground where black, wet rock seeps all the way down into darkness. A crack in the surface and the soft red sandstone that is so visible on the nearby beach has worn away. Beyond this, the way dips and then rises again and the soft, buoyant sedge is both luxuriant and sapping. It gives a bounce to the step but pulls back at the same time. This carpeted path now winds downwards; for it is here that the small headland lies. It is connected to the mainland by a slight, narrow neck of land. On either side the stone tumbles away to the sea and to rocks that spend a share of their time beneath water. To the right there is the trace of a path, perhaps an old fishing route, a square patch of shingle lying at the bottom. No one comes here now, though, and I have never come across a single soul on these cliffs. Not so long ago a farmer I met on the lane said of even twenty years ago that there were often visiting children up here. But no longer, he said; no one comes now. Many, many years ago though there would have been a lot of human activity up here, for standing on the narrow connection of land there is still visible on the path up to the promontory the remains of a building. Standing there now, surrounded by sea on a small jut of land, it is hard to believe that there once stood here a fortress castle said to be over forty feet in height. Said to have been built by a clan specialising in putting up 'strongholds in inaccessible, perilous positions along the coast',[10] its residents were ejected in 1642. A band of stone along the eastern entrance is all that seems to remain now, the only evidence of the workings of human hands, but the inaccessible plateau, the sward-covered island remains.

The sedge is like a carpet, the grass tough and thick. The Atlantic lies out in the distance as far as the eye can see. There is always sound from the ocean and yet the most striking thing about sitting on the grass is the silence, the absence of noise, as if the sound that is there is so much in context that it is heard in a different way. Surrounded by the unending noise of wave and cliff-side, the deep bass-like booms from far beneath, the realisation comes of how rare silence now is and how this noise is so fitting to the ear. Perhaps, in harmony with its surroundings it barely registers as noise at all. Seán Ó Faoláin wrote once of an Ireland that had 'the same silent night for miles about, far beyond the town, in the cabins glimmering among the moist fields, always the same for mile after mile through the whole length and breadth of Ireland, a gentle, dim night where only the small sounds murmured in the grass and the dark and oncoming sleep muffled human speech'.[11] It is likely that for most of us that kind of silence is now as rare as the corncrake who used to so mercilessly punctuate it.

I have watched the gannet that plummets into the sea for a few minutes in the hope that it will dive, and it eventually does. The speed and ascent of the entrance into the water is tremendous, with dives said to take place from heights of anything of between 50 and 100 feet. At the last moment, with the head already appearing to be in the water, the wings close and the bird goes under. This pelagic bird, spending most of its life out at sea, travels huge distances every day to feed and the bird I watch nests on either Bull Rock or Little Skellig, both miles and miles away. The colony at Little Skellig is said to be home to an astonishing summer breeding population of over 20,000 pairs of gannets. Their dives, often accompanied by a final twirl, are a sight to behold and though the bird is sleek and coldly dynamic, it has an austere beauty. Roderic O'Flaherty writing in the 1680s watched the gannets too. Unlike Giraldus, O'Flaherty was not a visitor to the country and his observations were far likelier to have been more extensive and to have had a greater depth. He died in poverty, in 1718, with the religious upheavals of the years before having seen him lose immense tracts of land. Yet he watched and wrote of the Irish landscape and standing perhaps on a headland like this, he saw some 300 years ago what I see now. 'Here the ganet soares high into the sky to espy his prey in the sea under him, at which he casts himself headlong into the sea, and swallows up whole herrings in a morsel. This bird flys through the ship's sailes, piercing them with his beak.'[12]

Roderic O'Flaherty travelled extensively throughout Ireland, as did Giraldus some 500 years before him, but in the time between them nobody else recorded anything of any great detail about the Irish environment. Yet both men would have garnered much of what they did by writing down the observations of others and this relative silence when it comes to nature is probably more to do with writers being concerned with other things, theology in particular, than with widespread ignorance. It is likely, in fact, that a close and detailed relationship with nature was widespread, whatever gaps there are in our recorded knowledge. In Ireland, though, the holes in our knowledge are not just ones between contemporary scholarly concerns and those of the past but between an Irish-speaking country and an English-speaking one. Not only, like other countries, have we lost elements of the past because they went unrecorded but in our case because there was once a community whose relationship with nature was conducted through the medium of another language. As the poet Aidan Mathews puts it, 'The tide gone out for good/Thirty-one words for seaweed/ Whiten on the foreshore.'[13] Or as Michael Viney writes 'the intimacy with nature that the "old people" knew has, indeed, been overtaken by a sort of silence'.[14] The way that a whole society conducted itself in relation to the natural world is now estranged from us and in a very large way this is because it was conducted in a different language.

When the choughs appear it is their high-pitched call, their unchanged language, that slowly alerts me, a strangely light call for a crow. Here in Ireland the chough is a scarce enough coastal species but on our neighbouring island it is virtually absent. In England there are thought to be only two pairs and so restricted is its range that it is even called the Cornish Chough. Our population is far more substantial, amounting to as many as 2,400 birds. In fact Ireland has around 60 per cent of the population for the whole of northwestern Europe, the bird appearing on our coastline more than anywhere else in Europe. Still, because of their relative scarcity, their special status, I somehow expect the choughs to be sombre, serious creatures, as if they might in some way realise. They, of course, do not. They are, instead, slightly comical, clown-like birds; along with the high call their red beaks and claws give them the appearance of wearing morning-after make-up. I recall once seeing them, not far from here, above a winter pier as the mist started to roll in and the day turned to night. The four choughs I had come across suddenly called and disappeared into the night, their sad red feet and legs, poignantly, just visible as they went. Though they are shy and supposed to have none of the pugnacity that characterises so many crows, they have, as I watch now, what seems like inherently playful lives. They dive head first over the ditches and into fields and the pair before me, monogamous and paired for life, tumbling over the machair, seem to chase and harass each other, taking turns with the different roles. Even their long soaring flight, interspersed with rapid wingbeats, resembles nothing so much as a child freewheeling a bicycle. Unless they are aware of some wider biological loneliness, they are quite clearly unaware of any scarcity surrounding their species, oblivious to any fragility surrounding their existence. Any sadness their red-fringed appearance might carry is merely the sadness of those at the end of the party but with the feeling that there is always another party coming.

That there are at least four recorded names for choughs in the Irish language says as much for the birds as it does for a society that lived so close to the natural world. It was called *Chathóg dheargchosach* in the Aran Islands, *Coróg* in west Mayo, *Cosdhearg* in Kerry and is listed as *Cág cosdearg* in the latest Irish bird guide.[15] This shows both the richness and complexity of a linguistic culture and the authenticity of a society's relationship with the natural world, both of which are quite startling to the modern mind. Of course, it also illustrates the point that when it came to categorising nature, that doing so through Irish might have presented fairly insurmountable problems. With some suggesting that names for species changed if a mountainous area was traversed or even a river crossed it is clear that 'the linguistic map of Gaelic nomenclature was clearly a fractured one, and even where the available names had been recorded there remained their application to the species known to science'.[16] Irish, we could say, was almost too rich. For the chough though, a bird some incidentally called the sea crow, a relatively rare European bird, there is simply the evidence of how well the country knew it.

There is much evidence to suggest that choughs, despite their uncommonness, are still present now in places where they have been for generations and, being all-year-round residents, probably live most of their life span within a relatively small area. They share this local fidelity with a close relative, the raven, a similarly sedentary species, which somewhat more darkly is also known to prey on chough nests. Not too far down this coast a pair of ravens can often be seen. Large, heavy birds, they are in many ways the opposite of the choughs in terms of their sombre appearance. Like the choughs, though, they too are faithful to each other and to a locality. Damien Enright writes of the ones on the nearby coast that 'they mate for life, and when a partner dies, a young bird immediately takes up its place, so that there is a continuum of ravens at the same site, never breaking the tenancy or the genetic chain. This raven family may have been there for a millennium.'[17] Powerful, strong birds, they are in many ways more striking than the choughs, more the bird of mythology and romance, like the wonderfully fast and explosive peregrine falcons that I have also seen a handful of times on this coast. Yet, despite the presence of these more impressive species, it is the chough, both elegant and clown-like, that is simply the most joyous to see. Whether it is their comedy, their high-pitched call or their scarcity, something of their fragility comes away with me.

As I leave, having sat for hours on the luxuriant thickness of the grass, the light has begun to fade and I make my way back slowly along the narrow path. Some kind of path would have existed along this cliff face for centuries, some way made by the passage of human feet, to and from castle, fishing site or farm wall. What I walk along could well be a desire path hundreds of years old, even here, right at the edge of the island. I notice as I pass that, on the rock below, the gulls and the cormorant, joined now by a lesser black-backed gull, have sat too. Not eating, not drinking, engaging in nothing animalistic, simply sitting and looking out to sea as I have done. I feel the moisture seeping through the air as I turn to go. There was no sign of any swallows.

Now it seemed logical to plunge into what Edward Thomas called the 'fifth element': the element of wood.[1]

Roger Deakin

3

The Fifth Element

With the swallows gone there is suddenly a day when the wind whips through trees that are nearly bare. For some reason, some over-imaginative, Gothic reason, this brings the ravens to mind. They are the birds of storm and autumn, birds of solid darkness, birds of grim mythology. They are also, less an-thropomorphically, a resident species, a big, dense bird that never leaves us. Something about that, with summer swallows departed, with leaves tumbling from trees, lends them a reassuring appeal. Simply, now that summer has left, the ravens can be relied upon because the ravens stay. Their presence is a fidelity that does not have to be marked by return.

One of the Irish names for Ireland was *Inis na bhfiodhbhadh*, the island of woods, a country that was heavily forested from coast to coast. I think of this as I set out to see the ravens. To reach their cliff-side site I must pass through a small village and then a small patch of woodland. The raven site is not far from the closely cultivated fields surrounding the farmhouse I leave from, in the vicinity of the next parish but being, again, so much closer to the sea, it is a very different habitat. The small, coastal village curves around the shape of the bay, embracing the natural contour of the coast. The obligatory new housing estates sit at either end. The village and the estates are like two unconnected areas, two places far away from each other. Along the village there is a narrow line of sandy beach running beside the older settlement and just off this is a path leading up to the woodlands. Beyond this I hope to find the very ravens that might possibly have lived there for a thousand years.

In autumn sunshine the sea to my left is deceptively calm. Past a few bungalows that face out across the water I take the grass path to the woods and see the tall, heavy greenness of the trees ahead. This is old, mixed-deciduous woodland and there are trees at odd angles, trees lying where they have fallen. It ascends up and away from the coast and has a lively irregularity about it, the irregularity so many wooded plantations lack. The seasons course through this wood:

> In spring, the forest floor is carpeted in bluebells, which climb the slope to the right in a haze of purple. White ransoms, smelling of garlic, and delicate wood anemones, which close in the evening, are other flowers of the woods. There are a variety of mushrooms in autumn, including blewits, parasols and russula, and beechmast and hazel nuts . . . Long eared owls nest in a tree hollow.[2]

I have seen this wood flooded with bluebells in spring, seen bees flocking around the honeysuckle, seen it sway in a coming Atlantic storm. Even now there is something about the woods, in the windblown lull between one season and the next, before winter proper bites in. Even now this small forest carries something intrinsically particular, something that reaches out. 'To enter a wood is to pass into a different world in which we ourselves are transformed,' wrote Roger Deakin.[3] So, for a moment, I stand still. I peer up and across at the thin canopy above me. I see the sky through gaps in the green. I listen to the wood. There is a different presence here. This is a different place. This space completely belongs to the trees. The wind passing through it, the ocean beside it, the birds moving in it, the water that makes its way past it, all of these things do so through the element of the wood itself. The forest is the first thing. I am beneath the height of the trees, the beech and the thin, elegant birch, the occasional oak. Two bare paths testify to man's presence through here but this is not a managed place. A discarded can of beer and the occasional flutter of litter can sometimes be found here but they signify more, where these trees are concerned, man's disregard, his absence rather than his intent. There is thick undergrowth on the forest floor and enough loose wildness to suggest man's interference here is at a minimum. Beneath the trees, nearly falling off the coast on one side, the nearby ocean is forgotten. The glimpse of blue sea from time to time is reduced to a simple backdrop. It is the trees that hold sway here. Their soft, sibilant noise. Their grandness. Their completeness. Something other is here. Something the surrounding land, where trees are confined to hedgerows or the occasional small stand, does not possess. There is something fundamental here. Jean Giono's wonderful parable, *The Man Who Planted Trees*, comes to mind; the shepherd covering acres of war-torn land with the promise of trees because it 'purifies and renews the earth about us, because it comforts us, and because it reconciles us to death'.[4] Something rudimentary, something elemental and indispensable is to be found beneath these tall specimens of the silent world. What can be touched here is simplicity, simplicity as an unadorned virtue. 'The simplicity of song but more often of silence, and always of life.'[5] And simply standing beneath the trees seems to be enough to realise this; that this can be found here beneath these trees, in this small patch of woodland, in a corner of southwest Ireland that is only steps away from the ocean.

What is really wondrous though, what is truly rich here, is the realisation of how diminished it all is. This small expanse of wood, carrying all that it does within it, is a mere flicker of what was once the dominant feature of this island. Ireland now has, whatever the impression those standing armies of conifers blocking the hillsides might give, one of the least amounts of tree cover in Europe. The island of woods is long gone. The forests of Ireland are now lost. So it is hardly surprising, even standing beneath the cover of this headland wood, that Frank Mitchell's words should ring so evocatively true and that it really is impossible for us to 'picture the majesty and silence of those primeval woods, that stretched from Ireland far across northern Europe'.[6] All of that is gone from us. In that sense the landscape carries with it a sense of loss and this is intensified in the realisation that, while what we call primeval or ancient woodland is something consigned to the vast stretches of the past, a forested Ireland is not. Even when man had begun to make extensive alterations to the aboriginal environment around him, even as the land began to be shaped by man's actions and original forest was cleared for fields and flocks, Ireland's tree-covered past survived well into documented, historical times. 'The extent and regenerative properties of the native forests were so great and powerful that, in spite of inroads of this and more intense kinds over the following thousand years, the greater part of the country even as late as the twelfth century was still clothed in trees.'[7] Even writing of the Ireland of as late as 1600 the historian Roy Foster is able to state that 'Irish woods were famous: varied, dense and impenetrable to the unfamiliar. Willow, birch, hazel, pine, alder, oak, elm and ash were predominant, though the concentration varied: yew woods in Cork, oak in the southeast.'[8] The picture is truly that of a vanished environment, a heritage of forest, lost.

The destruction, when it came, came fairly rapidly and came not haphazardly but coherently. Irish woodland was felled for a variety of considered reasons; economic, cultural and military. Irish trees had been felled over the years as man's activities extended into forested areas but the final removal of the old tree-covered Ireland came about deliberately and intentionally. 'The systematic devastation of Irish woodlands followed rapidly on the unexpected defeat of the combined Irish and Spanish forces at Kinsale in 1601. As a result the substantially forested Ireland of 1600 had by 1711 become a treeless wilderness and a net importer of timber.'[9]

How much this must have changed the basic physical appearance of the country can only be imagined. If we have to struggle to picture Ireland's vast forests we can barely glimpse what their destruction must have looked like. This was forestry clearance on a grand, commercial scale and with a government survey as late as 1623 reporting that Ireland abounded in good timber, at a time when timber was one of the prime goods of the world, the equivalent of today's oil, it is easy to see how ripe the environment of the newly colonised country was for wholesale exploitation. The removal of the forests would have affected every corner of the country, would have been felt by all those living here. 'These half-felled woods were to be seen everywhere, even in the furthest places; there was, for instance, a great clearance made at Coolmountain in West Cork.'[10] That area is not too far from here, from the trees under which I now stand, and is to this day a remote corner. It seems unlikely that many living here would have been untouched by such a fundamental alteration to their environment. Likewise, David Dickson writes of a great tract of land in this corner of Ireland that in the 1680s was still 'a large wooded country' and that in the '1650s there had been over 8,500 acres of woodland in the barony. However, by 1714 . . . it was claimed with only slight exaggeration that not one acre of old timber remained.'[11] Even if there was no culture involving these forests, it was landscape alteration on a truly astonishing scale, especially in a non-industrial age. Another aspect of this first of the landscape traumas would have been, of course, not just the disappearance of the forests but of the myriad species of wildlife that existed within them; the deer and the goshawk, the wolf. All of these would have gone into a sudden decline. The physical environment of Ireland would have been altered beyond recognition. The whole natural world of the island would have been drastically different within the living memory of society. When the trees went, a whole biological existence, a whole ecological framework, went with them. What also departed, of course, was a way of being in Ireland, a cultural existence that was tied in with the natural world of the island in a way that is, once more, hard for a modern sensibility to grasp. The felling of the forests was not just a material clearance; it was a cultural one, too. There was more than physical lumber taken from the land. For a people living on that land, in every sense of the word, their existence was such that it is not hard to believe that 'they would have held the trees, mountains and other parts of the landscape in reverence'.[12] They existed within the framework of their immediate environment. The way they behaved and thought existed within the context of that environment. When 'everywhere the giant woods were being cut down',[13] this way of thinking was being cut adrift too. The whole physical landscape was being altered beyond recognition and the entire mind of the society entwined with it was being utterly changed as well. Declan Kiberd writes that years later the remnants of this society still remembered this loss and even well into the 1700s one could still have heard the 'field labourers sing the great Gaelic lament for fallen forests, *Cill Cháis*.'[14] *Cad a dhéanfaimid feasta gan adhmad?/Tá deireadh na gcoillte ar lár.* Now what will we do for timber,/with the last of the woods laid low?'[15] The song mourns a way of life as much as it mourns the forest. The land, as those living on it would have realised, was being cleared not only in a material sense but metaphorically too.

That other way in which the woods were cleared is also a symbol of the way in which the Irish thought about the forests, for as their world changed around them in the early 1600s, the woodlands became their refuge; the trees became 'gathering places of opposition',[16] for what was, in effect, a defeated culture. The disappearing remnants of a collapsing society sought out the disappearing remnants of a collapsing environment. The new society that was arriving was well aware of this. It became such that, to the new settlers on the new Irish landscape, the woodlands and the Irish were inseparable, to the extent that Irish soldiers, reduced to seeking out the forests as their last refuge, became known as 'woodkernes'. In the same regard they became synonymous with that other symbol of the forests, the wolf. In the imagination of the Ireland that was replacing them they became intertwined, the woodkerne and the wolf. Elizabeth I duly ordered that, apart from the economic aspects of felling, the woods be cleared to deprive the Irish and the wolf of this very shelter. The days of both the forested Ireland and the wolf were now numbered, and the name of the Ireland that went with it, too. The war waged on Irish soil became as much a war against the trees, against the Irish environment, as it was against anything else. The inhabitants of the island and the environment became as one.

It is little wonder that a society living on a heavily wooded island had developed a sensibility closely entwined with that natural context. It is little wonder that they had a folklore and set of beliefs around that natural context. It is little wonder that they sought it out as their last refuge. What is a wonder though, is that within a short passage of time all the ideas of Ireland, of natural Ireland, of authentic Ireland would be those of a country without trees. The forests were no longer a part of the daily environment, they were no longer even the places of despairing refuge. In the light of all that went before, in the light of Ireland as the island of woods, of the woods as the last resting place of a defeated Irish culture, it is startling to realise that within 200 years ideas of Irishness had changed so much, in a biological context at least, that trees were now seen as foreign. There was a 'general hostility' to woodlands and 'mutilation and cutting of trees became a common form of protest'.[17] The lost forests had gone from being an intrinsic part of the culture of the island and from being synonymous with the Irish themselves to being thought of as belonging to an imposed ascendancy class. The poet Austin Clarke put it very simply and clearly in his poem 'The Planter's Daughter': 'For the house of the planter/Is known by the trees.'[18] In a remarkable twist of biological history woodland had now become synonymous with the newly arrived settlers, who began planting once they had finished clearing. With forests decimated the psychology of the island had turned fully around. The Irish were no longer lamenting fallen trees; they were 'mutilating' standing ones. So it was, that the archetypal image of the Irish landscape became that of the austere beauty of a green, treeless one. So it was that the splendour of an expansive, unbroken, sweeping Connemara became the standard example of what Ireland truly looked like. So it was that those who sought a cultural revival of Ireland in the early 1900s turned to that western seaboard as the genuine and authentic embodiment of what constituted Irishness. It was as if the destruction of the great forests had not only erased them from the material, physical landscape but also from the nurturing recesses of the Irish mind.

The distraction in these woods in which I stand is that they carry the echoes of all that history. These woods are old but they are planted. They are probably part of the old Earl of Shannon estate, part in themselves of the traumatic history of forests on this small island. In the earlier days of forest clearance the Boyles, the Earl of Shannon family, were eagerly involved in the profitable timber industry and at a time in the early decades of the 1600s when Cork was exporting 'vast quantities of hardwood barrel staves' the family recorded 'private transactions involving some four million staves'.[19] They were clearing away the forests of Ireland, clearing the forest from this corner of the island. Yet, following the path of other planter families, this and other woods were planted by a Boyle descendant at a time when, even before the 1600s had elapsed, the very same sections of society that had removed the great forests were expending huge amounts of capital on horticulture, landscaping and trees. Natural-style parks soon came into vogue with a 'new appreciation that "natural" features, such as woods, streams and hills, were beautiful in themselves and indeed good for the soul'.[20] What had been taken away was now thought of as the most advantageous to put back in and now that nature had been tamed it was to be regulated and given discipline and order. The landscape, in this way of viewing it, is always a blank canvas, awaiting realisation. There is, of course, the old colonial element here too, of something, in this case the land, having no intrinsic value until 'discovered'; even if that discovery involved denuding and then replenishing with the very same thing that was first taken away.

This woodland is a part of all that. Of all that destruction. Of the change of forest from intrinsically Irish to intrinsically foreign. This woodland is a palimpsest: layer upon layer of the Irish past beneath the trees. Once settlers like the Earl of Shannon began their replanting enterprises, of which this wood is, almost certainly, originally a part, the trees took on a different symbolic existence on the island. They were not now characteristic of the wooded island itself but characteristic of the demesne. Outside the demesne, Ireland was usually recorded in the same way, 'a dreary waste where, there is scarcely a twig sufficient to form a resting place to the birds fatigued with their flight'.[21] Trees became things that were confined to a certain place, a certain physical and cultural place. They were now seen, by their planters at least, as signs of improvement and superior culture. Then, in a circular sense early Irish artists might have recognised, the demesne trees too came up against man's political, cultural and economic design. Once Ireland's Free State came into being the demise of the demesne was not far behind, as the old ascendancy land became unsustainable for a declining economic and political class. The demesne estates were sold off and the woodlands met a now familiar end. 'By the 1920s Ireland's woodland had shrunk, from 340,000 acres in 1880, to about 130,000 acres.'[22] Much of that was to do with the break-up of those old estates. Not far from here, further back up the coast, in the grounds of a still standing, Gothic old demesne there is a walk to be taken amongst acres of wooded land. It is mainly conifer plantation now. Mary Carbery, the wife of Lord Carbery, kept a reflective, moving and sometimes beautiful diary of her time living there between 1898 and 1901. She writes deeply of the woods there, of their variety and their 'greening beech trees' and 'indescribable loveliness'. Those woods are gone now, replaced by a monotone plantation. Wooded Ireland had reached another stage.

But these woods themselves, although so much a part of that change, are also beyond it. They occupy another space that stands apart from that of the emblematic, beyond that of lost worlds or considerations of Ireland's material legacy. While it is hard to ignore the steady procession there has been through the space and time of our wooded landscapes, something that has created the places of today, none of it, for this moment, holds sway. For this moment, as I stand beneath these trees, this space is just itself and for this time it is just the woods and me. It is the life of the wood that I can see and hear and feel. Mary Carbery, so moved by her own woodlands, wrote from her neo-medieval home on a headland of the remote west Cork coast at the turn of the twentieth century, that 'isolation means a deeper love and sense not of possession, but of being a part of something essential'.[23] I recall her words now as I stand beneath the trees, as I listen, as I walk through them. Something in the woods is essential, something calls our steps on. For we have always been amongst trees. They are amongst the largest, longest-lived things on our planet. Through most of human life our fortune has gone hand in hand with theirs. The noise they now create, as the wind rises, is one that most of our ancestors would have had as the primary noise of their lives. There is the unavoidable, unscientific sense that they have some kind of sensibility, some sort of sentience. An awareness. There is a comfort in being here, in standing beneath them, in walking through them. Something that comes from them, from their physical presence. The trees bring us back. They root us. Though it is many generations since humans on this island lived amongst them to any great extent there is still the unadorned sense, standing beneath them, of being at home.

Reliably, heavily, the ravens are here. It would be hard to miss them. These largest of the crows are an impressive size and they have an obvious sturdiness about them. As I come out on the path that runs beside the coast the solidity of the raven stands out amongst the flight and movement of other birds. Sitting high in the branches of a cliff-side gorse the single bird I come across makes no attempt to hide or disappear. Though it is said that they are a bird that has not, unlike other crows, adjusted well to civilisation and are found instead in these wilder, uninhabited places, this is clearly not accompanied by any timidity. This bird seems almost arrogant, or at the least completely unperturbed by my presence, though there is the watchful awareness to be expected from any intelligent crow. I stare out to sea for a while and when I turn back the bird is still perched in full view impassively. The raven, a long-established European species, now occupies only a portion of its former range but their reassuring presence here reflects their ancient status. 'Around 2000 BC Ravens kept company with other Neolithic birds',[24] their history states, so it does not seem particularly far-fetched to imagine this territory as being occupied by an unbroken tenancy of ravens. They have been around us for a long time, long embedded in man's imagination. It is also true that individual birds have been recorded as enjoying a lifespan which exceeds that of most others. Though their lives in the wild are unpredictable, tamed ravens have lived for up to fifty years, with one individual purportedly living to a remarkable sixty-nine years of age. Though this is most unlikely, if not impossible in the wild, it is still an astonishing age for a bird. When I turn back again after watching the endless ocean, the bird is impassively sitting there. They are territorial, the guidebook says, and 'their mere physical presence is enough to stake a claim'.[25] Looking at the strong bird behind me I do not find that hard to believe. As far as the bird is concerned I get the impression we are looking out to sea as equals. There is, from time to time, the occasional gust of strong wind coming in from the ocean but the raven merely rides the rising of the branch the way a gull might sit atop a wave. Their plumage apparently has a purple or green sheen; however, I see nothing but unspoiled black. Recorded as nesting as early as January there is an unrelenting ruggedness about the raven. On the coasts it frequents it is thought of as the master of the air and even with the hardiness that most species on the fringe have it is not hard to see why that might be true. Like other corvids the ravens mate and stay together for life. The bird I observe now will probably spend its whole life along this patch of coast. Somehow all these factors, the antique status of the species, their possible longevity, their faithfulness to site and partner, their physical solidity, creates a reassuring presence. In his poem 'The Raven's Nest' the English poet John Clare wrote of this very thing. '. . . where still they live/Through changes winds and storms and are secure/And like a landmark in the chronicles/Of village memorys treasured up yet lives/The hugh old oak that wears the raven's nest.'[26] An enduring raven's nest becomes, in that sense, like a repository of our memory. Emblems of our mythology, these birds have always been around us and we around them and even though they have retreated now to these wilder, untamed, less bothered places, there is still a connection between us. The raven that sits now easily, almost playfully on the outcrop of gorse, above the spot where Damien Enright fancied a raven family might have been for a millennium, offers a connection with a previous country, a continuum when so much is being discarded that, as I stand here buffeted by Atlantic winds, is like an anchor. When there is, as now, such a disjuncture between society and the natural landscape it is something of a comfort that the raven, the master of the coast, is the master yet.

Making my way back along the path and coming up again to the beginning of the woodland I stop once more and look back. The sea stretches away from me. From where I stand on this windy, autumn day, I can see, far off in the distance, the furthest finger of land. It is now an exclusive golf club; but that headland is the Old Head of Kinsale and is the very same place where those Irish forces were defeated in 1601 and where the ultimate demise of the old Gaelic order can be said to have commenced. Soon enough, too, it marked the thorough and final clearance of the remaining Irish woodlands, a history the beautiful woods I am about to re-enter are so much a part of.

From the woods to the ravens and back again our memory is stored. It is cold now. The wind picks up and there is sea spray in the air. I seek the shelter of the trees.

'I have traversed Ireland to and fro from end to end, and from sea to sea. Mostly on foot, for that is the only way to see and get to know intimately any country.'[1]

Robert Lloyd Praeger

4

Perception's Pace

Another mysterious, hefty, symbolic species, once rare but now increasingly seen along the coast, the peregrine falcon, is in my mind sometime after the ravens and the wood. I know that they have been spotted not far from where I saw the ravens and I am drawn to go back that way in the hope of seeing them. Luckily, I have seen them once already along these coasts; a powerfully built, bulky bird flinging by on a cold afternoon. They are now, thankfully, a far commoner sight than they once were and I would like to watch them more closely. Find some hidden spot where I could observe them and they would not be disturbed by me. Still, with summer gone and autumn drifting steadily into winter, it is harder to stir from the fireside. At times it is easier to watch the world from the window or find it in the pages of a book. So I walk one day down the long lane from the farmhouse, half intending to set off. If I get there, I think, all well and good but if not there will be another time. I am leaving myself open to distraction. Hours later though, I find I have been nowhere near the coast, am not attempting to catch the wonder of a peregrine and have become lost instead in that basic, most simple, of activities. I have spent the hours I had put aside for the peregrines in walking.

Sometimes it can feel, especially perhaps in an Ireland that has undergone such spectacular change, that walking is something of a political act. By walking I do not mean the hurried walking that is designed to shed excess weight, the power walking that propels so many along the lanes and footpaths. I mean more the considered walk, the walk at 'perception's pace',[2] the walk, in many ways, without purpose. Henry David Thoreau writes most beautifully of this, even if there may be some doubt as to the veracity of his definitions. For him the art of walking is characterised by the word 'sauntering' and he explained the origins of that word in two equally enchanting ways. One was that it came from those people who roved about the landscape of the Middle Ages and asked for charity under the guise of going to the Holy Land. Eventually children began to say 'there goes a Sainte-Terrer', a saunterer. Or, he claims, it came from those who were *sans terre*, without land or home, who were vagrant, who, indeed, having no particular home were at home everywhere.[3] This was sauntering, walking the land almost for a living or walking the land as a way of being, depending on which of Thoreau's definitions you give most credence to. The art of that kind of walking may well now be lost, maybe even impossible in a different world, at least in the west but it is still true that until very recently the world for most people, not just people in certain geographical areas, was a walking world. Walking would have been the mode of transportation, the way of existing that was known to most people. For very many of them, indeed for the great majority, it would have been the only way of getting around. Walking as a pastime of the leisured class or as way of losing weight would have seemed very strange. Even the idea of thinking about walking may well have been unknown when walking was not a matter of choice.

It is not, though, the intellectual or spiritual ramifications of walking that most occur to me as I saunter down the lane: it is the fundamental physical experience of it. It is the intimacy that it inherently involves that is most apparent, even before I have gone any further than the lane itself. Having walked here before with the farmer whose lands adjoin this lane, having lingered here and spoken with him, I am able to look at some of the fields at hand and know their names, the simple everyday usage they were given by those who worked them and walked them and depended upon them. So I am able to look at High Field where the land folds sharply upwards, at Marsh Field where the reedy grass still belies the many drainings of it, and to pass the Well Field where water was drawn. Uncomplicated but invisible. Unrecorded names. I pass them all as I walk by and feel that this simple knowledge, this most recent naming of the land, brings me in some way closer to the grammar of the landscape, the trees and the flowers and the birds, the secret pools of water, the black streams and the stone outcrops. Even if I am, in all likelihood, following the historical precedence of recording them only as they vanish, in some small but telling way I have, by virtue of those names, a secret knowledge of what lies about me. It is not like walking with ghosts, though it is things from the past that I possess, but walking in a closer proximity to life. Walking this small expanse of land, this lane through fields, I am covering what has been on many occasions the near entirety of a life. The farmer whose fields these are has lived here all his life and his own father came up this lane in 1917 to take possession of this land. There is a continuity here. In Sean Sheehan's wonderful evocation of his uncle's life on a west Cork peninsula not too far from here, *Jack's World*, he writes that an 'afternoon's walk encompasses much of the natural world where Jack and his ancestors were born, where he lived all of his eighty-three years and where he died in the early summer of 2003'.[4] Likewise, the farmer who owns these fields has told me of the five-mile walk to and from school each day, along the long road, short-cutting through fields, making desire paths, coming back along this very lane. Life before motorised transport and for many years after its arrival was, by virtue of being on foot, lived within more immediate, more intimate geographical boundaries, at least in the day-to-day sense. The most keenly felt of these, from home place to field, are those I am walking now, those I am slowly crossing, those I am sauntering. The possession of the simple names they have most recently been given means that as I pass them I am able to recognise a glimpse of the way of life that not so long ago surrounded them. It means I am given some signpost into the particularities of the place, some hint of the direct experience of it. Some meaning that I would not have had. I am close, equipped as I am, to the full physical sensation of this lane. I can see it at my feet and I can see, beyond the ditches of gorse and old ash, the nature of the fields and the names they gave themselves.

In a physical sense it is the gorse that, even this late in the year, is the most striking. At the bottom of the lane one side of the ditch consists almost entirely of this hard, spiky, evergreen and whilst, as the seasons have moved on, everything else has died back, the gorse – or furze as it is locally called – still flourishes. There is an air of robustness, standing beside it, that is hard not to revel in. Thinking now of the tenacious, unforgiving nature of it, it is hard to imagine that there was a time when this plant was harvested as a winter crop for horses or that such was its worth it was cultivated from seed. There was even in use, in this part of rural Ireland at least, a furze-chopping machine that made the task of transforming it into fodder less backbreaking. Now, all these years later, it is more the tough presence of forgotten corners, of undeveloped wayside and lane, the ever present when everything else has seasonally retreated. Somehow too, it is as if the splatter of delicate yellow flowers that incongruously litter the bush are ever present, even though I know this is biologically incorrect. Still, it does not appear as if the bush is ever simply green. Now though, as I lean forward to the yellow flowers that do yet survive, the sweet coconut scent they carry in summer has gone. That is not a smell of the lanes at this time of year and, indeed, it is not a scent that is ever offered up easily. It is only on leaning in that the surprising sweetness of the gorse is discovered; a short, shallow hint. When I turn to the gorse in a botanical guide I am again told that it only flowers from February to May if it is the common gorse or from July to September if it is the more likely western gorse. None of that seems to fit the flowering pattern of the lane and indeed September has been and gone now and these flowers linger. Yet I wonder if it is just a misconception on my behalf, so used am I to seeing the yellow and I am aware again, as with the swallows, for instance, that what the natural world presents to us is then filtered through a myriad of assumptions and beliefs of our own. Our ability is limited. Our understanding inherently rationed. I am even failing to categorise this plant a few hundred yards from my backdoor. One truth I do discover for the gorse though is that, however tough it seems, it only really flourishes in a climate like ours; a damp, mild one. The hardy gorse flourishes because, as they might say here, so many of our days are soft.

There is more than this, though, for the gorse also reveals some of the hidden details of our landscape's narrative. Quite simply, the gorse has been put there on purpose. The impenetrability of the gorse meant that it was one of the species widely planted in hedgerows when enclosure began to gather pace after the disappearance of the forests. Around the time that the lost forests were being felled and the trees of a new society planted in their stead, hedge construction began in earnest and whilst enclosure and the loss of commons does not seem to figure so traumatically in the agrarian history of Ireland, as opposed to the central, nearly defining role it plays in the rural history of England, these thorny bushes are part of a wider story.

Hedgerow in Ireland primarily had its origin in marking the boundaries of townlands like this one I walk on, townlands that had more or less attained their modern being when a group of tenant farmers joined together to muster the gains from their leased land. Where this then leads us to is the generally unrevealed history that these hedgerows would have been part of a countryside that, when larger farmers wanted to expand, saw many of the smaller farmers and labourers who occupied these townlands, quite simply, in the way. Within these hedgerows, the conflict between agricultural labourers and cottiers on one hand and strong farmers on the other was played out, a conflict that historian Joseph Lee writes has 'been consigned to almost total oblivion in the popular mind'.[5] In that way this ditch of gorse and earth and stone and tall, indestructible ash, may tell of other reasons why the old parish record of this townland shows that decline from 227 people pre-Famine to just 79 after. And it may, by its very existence, show who benefited from this. For, as the old map also illustrates, the lane did not come this way in 1845. It was altered afterwards, when many of the souls living at the top of the townland had gone. As Joseph Lee again adds, 'there were winners as well as losers in the famine stakes'[6] and it may well have been the winners that, thinking of increase and not the subsistence acre for the potato, built up this ditch and the new direction of the lane. Patrick Duffy puts this sharply and bleakly when writing about enclosure in Ireland. 'Social relations which stood in the way of modernisation were at times ruthlessly obliterated. A study of such a landscape cannot be described in terms of an innocent transformation.'[7]

The tough, yet soft-climate-loving gorse confuses me with its flowers and offers me sad, dark, riddles as part of the landscape. Here, in the sudden shade, the lateness of the year reminds me of how cold it has become.

I walk on. All the forgotten stories are on my mind. Patrick Duffy, again, has written of 'elite narratives' of the landscape and of how many of these there are compared to the paucity of 'records about ordinary places occupied by ordinary people'.[8] I think of this, not only because of the rugged, confusing gorse in the hedgerow at the bottom of the lane and what this might be telling me about those who lived in what is now my own backyard, but because of another place that comes to mind as I reach the end of the lane. Not too far from here, maybe two or three miles on what is now the main road to the city and the spreading suburbs of Cork there is, a small distance back from the road, a stone-built, two-windowed ruin. The roof is gone and it is merely the durability of the stone and the skill of those vanished builders that keeps it standing. The grass grows around it and through it and the bramble clogs its openings. It is the postcard scene of the Irish ruin, beloved of the emigrant; 'one more payment and it's mine', the caption might read. At least until recently there were many like it in the Irish landscape. One time I asked the owner of that land if he knew anything about it, anything of who it might have once housed. He looked at it as if he had forgotten it was there. I think, he said, someone who once worked for my father around the farm lived there. He shrugged. I do not know where he went, he added.

At the bottom of the lane as I reach the long vista of the straight road I hesitate. Cars here are infrequent but some of those that pass do so at high speed. I turn back to look up the lane. For once the understated, beautiful stonechat is not perched on top of the gorse or the telephone wire above it, flicking its wings and tails constantly. Neither is its sharp song to be heard, the one likened to the sound of stones clicking together, the one giving the bird its name. Whenever I walk this lane I am accustomed to seeing it; it is usually on top of the gorse and may even make its nest amongst those spines. It seems true, too, that the more regular the walker the less notice some species take, just as the walker may be taking more. The stonechat, though often seeming restless, never appears disturbed by my passing or my lingering or my talking nearby with the farmer. Perhaps, this is how urban birds can become so unaffected by human presence, the sheer volume of traffic making them immune. A few days ago, coldly waiting by a small bridge in the nearby town, I stood beside the local Spar, across from a building site where ambition seemed to grow brick by brick, higher and higher into the sky. Morning traffic passed slowly by. I turned to the water beneath the bridge and noted the bottles and the rubbish. I noted too, after a short while, the dipper slowly making its way up the water. It patrolled the water's edge and was obviously at home here in its urban waterway. I did not get to see it walking beneath the surface as I have seen it do elsewhere but I did watch its plump, white-banded body moving knowingly amongst what, to my eyes, was an unpromising stretch of water. The bird, though, was uninterested in the supermarket, the traffic, the building site, or the floating rubbish. Even though it is supposed to be found along fast-flowing rivers and to prefer upland regions, what most struck me about this bird, in a coastal, urban, slow-moving stream, was the fact that the dipper is an Irish subspecies.

With this island having been fully isolated from other land masses for over 8,000 years our relatively few breeding species, in comparison again to our nearest neighbour, are compensated for, amongst other things, by some distinct Irish races. In essence these species have had no interaction with any other European species for all that time and have gradually developed characteristics particular to this small island. So the dipper in the littered water outside the Spar has subtle differences from a British bird from across the Irish Sea. I cannot see those differences on that cold morning, the smaller chestnut band below the white or the slightly darker upper parts, but simply knowing they are there cheers me. Or, to be more honest, I am cheered by the dedication and knowledge, the attention, that has gone in to knowing these differences exist at all. The loving observation. That someone has noted the Irish dipper, the jay, the coal tit and the red grouse are different from their environmental counterparts, in far from obvious ways, somehow warms my wait.

On the long, straight road I move slowly on. With a substantial estate or demesne over the brow on one side and an old church and rectory on the other, it is clear that this road would have been one of the improved thoroughfares of the eighteenth century, when the rising wealth of a certain class meant they extended their control of the land outwards. Chances are, though, with a village at either end of it, an old

McCarthy castle in ruins away over to the left and the main road to Cork at the fork of one end, that the improvements of the new road are merely laid down upon the old folkway of a previous age. The truth is, that apart from the brutally new, the flyover or the motorway, most of our roads have an older origin than they might at first reveal. We move along routes dreamed of and worn in by our ancestors. Our roads are often, even in a strictly material way, 'the sum of our pasts, generation laid over generation, like the slow mould of the seasons'.[9] We may walk alone but we have company. A few coastal headlands along from where I saw the raven, for instance, some thousand people once set out on a walk that had a completely different character from this stroll of mine. In 1602, a year after the defeat at Kinsale and before the wholesale felling of those remaining forests, the chieftain Donal Cam O'Sullivan Beare took his clan away from their southwest peninsula in an attempt to reach the asylum of O'Neill lands some 250 miles to the north. During what was a bitterly cold winter they walked for fifteen days and fought skirmishes along the way with both Crown forces and other hostile Irish clans. When they finally reached a place of safety, somewhere near what is now County Leitrim, only thirty-five of them remained alive. They walked to their end. Likewise, sometime during the Famine, a group of people set off to walk ten miles of wild, bleak Mayo countryside from the town of Louisburgh, along the shores of Doo Lough, to plead with Poor Law officials for help. When they reached their destination the officials were 'at lunch and would not be disturbed, so the soaked and starving people were left to wait amongst the pine trees. When the two gentlemen finally came out they refused the people relief and told them to make their way back to Louisburgh.'[10] On the night walk back all 400 of the starving people died. They walked, too, to their end. It may well, in fact, be true that an awful lot of walking in Ireland is walking in the footsteps of those others and in particular of Famine victims and that even the invisible remnants of history, if we stop, can be sensed.

The difference with our roadways now, though, is that most people do not walk them. Cars travel them and the evidence of that is always to be found by the walker. If I were to line up the species of roadkill I have seen, even merely over the last few years, I would easily cover the width of this straight road. I'd have the usual suspects: dog, cat, fox, badger, hedgehog, rabbit. The unlucky: rook, blackbird, frog. The markedly unusual: otter, stoat, pygmy shrew, coal tit, long-eared owl. I remember some distinctly. The very young fox cubs seen playing in the mist just a few nights before, the broken low flying blackbird, the perfectly formed, unmarked stoat, the still beauty of the owl. Cars take an incredible, silent toll and I think, too, appalled, of the millions of people who die because of them and wonder about the price we are willing to pay just to get from one place to another a little more quickly, hermetically sealed, absent even as we pass by. In a car we are removed from the world around us. As a great Irish walker once wrote, cars do not help you to see the land, they only enable you 'to leave it behind'.[11]

No cars pass me now though and I walk along with only the wind and the sound of cattle in a nearby field. I glance ahead and see a copse of trees by the old schoolhouse, where crows seem to gather throughout the day. This stand of tall sycamores, this non-native, resilient, usurping species with that strangely dirty bark, echoes with the call of the sociable crows as I near, even now when winter has quietened all the other species. For all of the busy, boisterous presence of the crows, though, and the jackdaws and rooks, what occurs to me is how sparse life actually is out in the fields. I am walking through absence. The idiosyncratic English politician and journalist William Cobbett wrote, in 1826, of travelling through the English countryside on horseback and coming across 'more goldfinches than I had ever seen together . . . They continued to fly along before me, for nearly half a mile, and still sticking to the road and the banks, I do believe I had, at last, a flock of ten thousand flying before me.'[12] Not in some prelapsarian, pristine Ireland but within the short time span of human activity was there an Ireland that was far more abundant in wildlife than the Ireland we have now, more abundant simply in terms of sheer numbers? Was there a time when there was just more of things? Whatever records we have, we obviously have nothing approaching a census count, but could the North American stories of skies black for days with passenger pigeons or thundering for days beneath bison have had some kind of equivalent here? Could there have been a time when the natural state held the truth of Louis MacNeice's words: 'World is suddener than we fancy it/World is crazier and more of it than we think.'[13] Or is this silence, this absence of obvious life, is this the natural state? Is that really likely?

As I walk on I am aware, too, that I walk in the footsteps of many others who have examined small corners of the world, have rooted around in forgotten places, and in an Irish context that many have walked the lanes, the roads and the byways, and written down the experience for those of us who would come after them. I think as I go of Padraic O'Conaire wonderfully, carelessly, traipsing across Ireland. Or the great Patrick Kavanagh setting off to walk from his Monaghan farm to Dublin city whilst trying to become an artist. Or more of one. Of others I have read, too, and think of them now as they rest amongst the pages of quiet obscurity. Of Amhlaoibh Ó Súilleabháin's closely detailed observations, in the Irish language, of the natural world around Kilkenny in the 1830s.[14] Of how intensely he must have experienced it. Of how he must have walked it. Of J. P. Burkitt lovingly ringing robins in his Fermanagh back garden in the 1920s and 1930s and worrying that he might be 'more interested in the created than the Creator'.[15] Of Ellen Hutchins who lived a short life not too far from where I walk and who, despite ill health, recorded in great detail such specialised plant life around her Bantry Bay home that a number of species now bear her name.[16] And I think also, of course, of Robert Lloyd Praeger and his 'way of flowers and stones and beasts'.[17] Praeger was one of Ireland's greatest walkers and his walks, so productive in terms of the knowledge he gleaned from them, that he is nearly cover enough for my own aimless meandering. My sauntering.

What all of these people did, though, was to turn their eyes on the seemingly insignificant, the neglected, the minutiae of the ordinary and in Praeger at least did so with a firm belief that walking was the only way such things could be studied profitably. Still, I would be dishonest if I were to pretend this walking of mine has been deliberate or structured. I have lacked intent. I have merely walked and at times I have stood and listened. And at times I have stopped and considered. The often severe Thoreau might, surprisingly, be my ally in this context. 'I sat in my sunny doorway from sunrise till noon, rapt in a reverie, amidst the pines and hickories, and sumachs, in undisturbed solitude and stillness, while the birds sang around or flitted noiseless through the house, until by the sun falling in at my west window . . . I was reminded of the lapse of time.'[18] No sun falls for me now on this cold, heavy day and I turn back towards my fire as, I suppose, people have always done. The peregrines will have to wait for another day.

Nature is not a place to visit, it is home.[1]

Gary Snyder

5

The Shared Experience

I sit by the fire awhile and read Robert Lloyd Praeger. Such was the breadth and extent of his work that it is almost impossible to think about the natural world in Ireland without referring to him. Fittingly enough he tells an interesting story about ravens and peregrine falcons, observed on this occasion whilst fighting each other. 'The falcon was the attacker, stooping fiercely on his opponent time after time and screaming incessantly. The raven countered his attacks by flying silently round and round in a wide circle a few feet above the ground, keenly watching his adversary.'[2] In the end it is the raven that, surprisingly, injures the peregrine, though both birds are then observed flying off. I feel even more now that the trip to the woods and to the raven has somehow led me on to the peregrine and knowing that they are even closer to here than the ravens, I know that I must go to the cliffs. The truth is, though, that I still linger, these hardy days, by the fire. I read instead and Praeger is soon mentioning, this being sometime in the 1940s, that the peregrine, mainly a bird of the cliff-side, had bred in 'recent times' in Dublin city centre. I cannot help thinking, staring into the fire, how, bearing this kind of aside in mind, the peregrine falcon has acted out, in microcosm, much of the distorted relationship between the natural world and man.

Due to its beauty, its agility, its speed and its deadliness, the peregrine has long held a totemic place in the human imagination. Some have even gone as far as suggesting that any attempt to write of the bird is now redundant, as every superlative has already been used in describing it. It is no surprise to learn then that the peregrine was the bird of choice at a time when falconry was the pastime of a wealthy, powerful, section of society. There was a time when peregrines exchanged hands for a lot of money. Such, indeed, was the status of the species, that some of the first conservation legislation enacted, probably by the same Hiberno-Normans who had first introduced hunting from the fist, was in order to preserve the haunts and nesting sites of such a sought-after bird. Some of those nesting sites are now thought to have been continuously occupied for hundreds of years, given that they were once protected and are still used now. Somehow, it seems ironic that even this bird, with its disturbed, often persecuted history should also carry such a strong link with fidelity to place, carry such a promise of consistency. Will those birds I hope to see on the cliffs be occupiers with a long heritage? Could they, too, be centuries-long residents like the ravens, a mere few miles from them? Could they be faithful, in their own manner, like the swallows now so far away? Or is that, in fact, unlikely, considering what befell a bird once, so valued, so protected? For when falconry fell out of favour and a certain section of society discovered hunting with guns instead, the peregrine falcon's prized status quickly disappeared. Now the bird, still of course a superb hunter, became a nuisance and a threat, a competitor. Gamekeepers took to persecuting it with an onslaught that was 'waged with unremitting vigour'.[3] For hundreds of years peregrines were simply killed. They were systematically destroyed. What was once so prized was now completely despised. The persecution and much of that onslaught has now abated and the peregrine has recovered, but that recovery did not take place before the peregrine falcon went on to play a starring role in yet another chapter in the story of man's long, tangled estrangement from the natural world, one that can now be said to have helped give birth to contemporary ideas of ecology and environmentalism. Rachel Carson's *Silent Spring* became one of the essential examples of nature writing in that it was the first time a scientist questioned the use of agrochemicals and pesticides, the use of which had increased rapidly after the end of the Second World War. Carson pointed out that what was supposed to kill insects that were damaging crops was 'spreading through the food chain'[4] and in that regard the 'story of the peregrine is particularly significant'.[5] In the 1960s, owing to the use of chemicals such as DDT, it was found that the number of peregrine falcons had collapsed. It was discovered that their ingesting of the chemicals thinned the shells of their eggs and led to the eggs breaking in the nest. The peregrine falcon, even though it was found throughout the world, was placed on the Red Data Species List, a bird classified as facing global extinction. Carson's book, of course, helped to awaken the world to what had been happening and the peregrine did recover. In Ireland it is now only on the Amber List, which is for those of medium conservation concern, where it is joined by the kestrel, the starling, the house sparrow, the gannet, the chough, and the swallow. All of those are of conservation concern here in Ireland. The sheer numbers we must have lost if even the sparrow and the starling are now thought of as being in decline strikes me again. If even the swallow. I think once more of Cobbett's goldfinches flocking in their thousands before him and the quiet fields, by contrast, that surround me. Rachel Carson writes, too, of vast numbers being lost to poisoning in the 1960s, of 'huge bonfires on which the bodies of birds were burned'.[6] So I linger by the fire and wonder again if there was a sheer richness in numbers that is now lost. Barry Lopez, writing of North America as recently as the 1860s, says 'wildlife was so plentiful biological historians think the fauna of the Great Plains at this time was as rich as it had ever been anywhere in the world . . . No one knows how many animals were killed on the plains from, say, 1850 to 1900 . . . it is conceivable that 500 million creatures died.'[7] Was Ireland like that once? Was there a time when Ireland's fauna was as rich as it would ever be? When the island was covered in trees perhaps, or before the Elizabethan fellings, or when the swallows hibernated in the mud? Or even, perhaps, just a few generations past, when the primordial skein of the land was as yet undisturbed and intact. Is our age just an age of remnants? Is the peregrine falcon, persecuted and then poisoned, now merely a symbol of that?

A clear, dry day comes and I leave the fire. I take the bicycle this time to drop down the lane, gathering speed as I go. Not so long ago the bicycle was Everyman's mode of transport. Flann O'Brien satirised this wonderfully, darkly, hilariously in *The Third Policeman*, where one character having 'spent no less than thirty-five years riding his bicycle over the rocky roadsteads and up and down the hills and into the deep ditches', is molecularly 'halfway to being a bicycle himself'.[8] Patrick Kavanagh, by contrast, found the gift of a bicycle 'propelled him from sheltered adolescence into adulthood, enabling him to attend football matches in neighbouring parishes, join the posses of young men cycling to dances',[9] becoming one of the bicycles going by 'in twos and threes' on his way to declaring 'A road, a mile of kingdom, I am King/Of banks and stones and every blooming thing'.[10] From the 1930s onwards too, the dedicated staff of the Irish Folklore Commission journeyed throughout the country on bicycles, collecting and preserving the cultural and linguistic heritage of the island.[11] This humble mode of transport has even been seen by some as playing its part in the establishment of our very state. 'Organizers such as Mellows cycled astonishing distances in all weathers . . . The revolutionary role of the Irish-made "Lucania" bicycle, a particular boon to Irish-Irelanders trying to boycott British imports, has not yet been fully appreciated.'[12] There is always, it seems, company.

At the bottom of the lane I slow so as to enter the straight road carefully and come to rest by the gorse, still in flower. The stonechat briefly appears but at this time of year, being one of the few insectivores that stay here throughout the winter, the bird does not linger and disappears into the Marsh Field. As it flits away from the top of the bush I remember that the guidebooks tell me it is actually the appropriately named, summer visiting whinchat that prefers the company of gorse and I feel once more the reassuringly blurred boundaries of our knowledge. One book that did so much for birds though, Rachel Carson's book, comes to mind again as I look back at the gorse, for that book was deemed notable for at least two main reasons. Firstly, it gave a first modern airing to the idea that 'everything in nature is related to everything else'[13] and, secondly, it married science and literature. As I gaze at the yellow-topped gorse, remember its sweet coconut smell, I recall that there is also a surprising

Irish precedent for that latter quality, in the form of Oscar Wilde. Wilde would, of course, be far better known as our great aesthete rather than someone associated with the harshness of gorse, aestheticism itself described as being 'predicated on a swerve from nature'.[14] He was also, though, a great reader of science in his youth and his father was a practising scientist. So perhaps this passage from his prison letter *De Profundis* should not be so surprising after all. 'Linnaeus fell on his knees and wept for joy when he saw for the first time the long heath of some English upland made yellow with the tawny aromatic blossoms of the common furze; and I know that for me, to whom flowers are part of desire, there are tears waiting in the petals of some rose. It has always been so with me from boyhood.'[15]

The odd car passes but these roads, these back lanes and minor routes, are generally quiet. Often I can stop and hear again the surprising silence of the earth, the stillness before sound comes through, the movement in a ditch, the shifting of a branch, and always, always, the birds. I turn a bend and stop suddenly at a handsome cock pheasant dead in the road. Feathers still fly in the soft breeze and the car that hit him is, I would imagine, not long passed. Introduced many centuries ago, the pheasant is still a peculiarly exotic-looking bird. Thousands of them are still introduced into the countryside each year with the sole purpose of being shot and it is indeed such a commerce that once heralded the demise of the peregrine. Somehow though, even as I look at the dead bird before me, it is heartening that this brightly painted bird is also now a resident breeding species, found throughout the country in such numbers that it has reclaimed, and been reclaimed by, the wild. This bird would, no doubt, have been one of those making that echoing, choking call that so often carries across the fields in spring. One call I will not hear though is that of another so-called game bird, the grey partridge. Formerly, this bird was found throughout the island and even as late as 1972 it was recorded as nesting in all counties, yet by 2005 only 140 birds in total were thought to survive, all in a small area of County Offaly. Some decline had been noticed as much as a century earlier, suggesting some overarching frailty about the species but its near disappearance is still remarkable.

Something about these birds though, the game birds, seems to disconnect them from the concerns of many of those who watch or record birds. It is almost as if they are not considered 'real' birds, as if because they are hunted, are often mixed with bred, specifically released individuals, belong so much to the activities of a certain kind of countryside enthusiast, that they do not qualify as truly authentic. This is not, of course, generally about the birds themselves but about, once more, that recurring psychological filter, that inherent distortion through which we so often live with the natural world. In the case of the grey partridge, that shy, understated, seldom-visible bird, this is even more misplaced than usual in that this indigenous bird can tell us quite a lot about the natural history of our island.

The grey partridge belongs to a set of birds that are often called by the wonderful epithet of 'rough-country birds'. They are birds 'associated with old-fashioned agriculture, unfenced lowland and upland commonages and coastal regions; in general, uncultivated or abandoned corners of the countryside'.[16] Those comical, cliff-side choughs by the headland would be part of this group. These 'rough country birds' all declined with the coming of intensive, industrialised farming, with the arrival of crop spraying and pesticides, monocultures and the disappearance of wasteland. We can associate them now with the removal of those forgotten corners that gorse might occupy. With the arrival of sprays that thinned peregrine eggs. With this evocative song of loss.

> It is interesting how these birds echo the decline and (in some cases disappearance) of a group of plants, victims also to modern agriculture . . . Darnel, Fat Hen, Corn Cockle, Cornflower, Corn Marigold . . . Were it not for the recent discovery of Corn Cockle and Darnel on the Aran Islands, these plants, at one time as commonplace as the crops in which they grew, would have passed from our consciousness without so much as a whimper.[17]

All of these species, plant and bird, would have been 'in their element from the time of the first woodland clearances (for they would probably have been rare or local in the unmodified landscape) right up until the decline of mixed farming'.[18] So the bird I cannot see, the game species that is not quite a proper bird, one of the vanished birds whose call I cannot hear, may well have flourished here when the woodlands were first cleared, when the first farmers came, when the Elizabethans cleared great wooded tracks around here, when the ravens were in their occupancy and the swallows were hibernating in the mud, and the same bird fell away like the tumbling chough by the sea when the rough corners were filled in and the gorse that had been put in the hedge was pulled out and the pesticides arrived that took away the old plants and the insects and the peregrine's eggs. What is moving, too, about this lost bird, this Irish species that once nested in every county, that I see now only in pictures, can only now imagine, that now only survives in a reserve, is that even more than the swallow or the raven, it practised a geographical fidelity that no longer appears to have a place in the world. The guidebooks tell me that partridges are 'extremely sedentary and may pass their entire lives in just two or three fields'[19] and that much like the corncrake their call would have been an integral part of any rural soundtrack. What I am left with is the sensation that not only does the land reveal itself in layer upon interconnected layer but also that, disturbingly, so much of that land now seems to be a mere ghost of itself. What would Cobbett or Carson, Kavanagh or the Folklore Commissioners, Praeger, Hutchins or Ó Súilleabháin, what would they think if they were on this road with me now? Would they wonder where everything has gone? Would they see only loss? I think as I wheel away that I have lingered too long on this road and that the seasonal cold has found me and I have looked across at fallow, stubble fields and fallen into seeing a bird that is not there.

The peregrine is there. The land drops down to the estuary as I approach and I am freewheeling in the breeze. The broad basin of the river is on my right, making its way to the sea, and beside me on the left is the beginning of the upward curve that is the cliff-side. On the other side of this is the wide bird-filled estuary but the peregrine's favourite haunt is the disused quarry. Large slabs of rock lie broken at the bottom of a sheer face and gorse grows amongst the scree. At an old entrance the quarry is now chain-fenced, to prevent further dumping, one assumes. As I look I see that the whole of this approach, here by the quarry and across the road by the river, is swollen with gorse. The yellow-topped display lights up the roadway but fails to keep out the cold truth of these early winter days. I peer over again at the sheer ledges of the quarry and see, in the distance, the slate-blue back of the peregrine against the slate-blue of the stone.

Birds of prey hold a particular fascination. However

much the sight of a kestrel hovering is still a common one, falcons and hawks and owls always have that air of otherness about them. Living in the city many years ago I regularly saw a pair of kestrels that nested in a school tower at the top of the street. Once, waiting coldly at a bus stop, I saw a ground-foraging group of sparrows across the road suddenly scatter as a kestrel landed amongst them. For a few moments the falcon remained on the concrete pavement and then disappeared across the houses and pubs at great speed. Likewise in cities across the Irish Sea I have heard, even on the streets of the inner city, the ghostly yet somehow comforting call of the tawny owl, an owl sadly absent from our own shores. On another occasion, in the countryside of northern France, I waited on a cool, damp summer's evening outside a barn to see the flying out of a barn owl, the huge face and the warm beauty of it still in my mind's eye. Back here, too, from my own doorstep one night, the beautiful, still body of the long-eared owl I found on the straight road at the bottom of the lane, those movements I thought I might have seen in the dark suddenly taking on a corporeal substance. The long tuft of the 'ears', the otherworldly orange eyes. The sharp, frozen claws. Then there was the winter a few years ago when a short-eared owl appeared in the field beyond the farmhouse. Twice at night it flew across the front of the house and most distinctively was seen one cold afternoon on the ground on the lane itself, the stocky presence soon taking off across the fields with slow, long, wingbeats. Something particular about them stays with me, something separate from other birds, something unlike the other sights from nature's doorstep. The fox reminds me of a hungry dog, the stoat too lithe and sinewy to linger long, the otter something from an unknowable, wetter place. The birds of prey and the owls, though, carry their own qualities, something, for all their speed and agility, of stillness and concentration that other flightier, more restless birds do not possess. Even the way they move seems to be from a different, self-defining place.

Yet, for all that, I was somehow prepared to be, if not disappointed, then at least somewhat unmoved by the peregrine. I was thinking of something the American poet Gary Snyder had written. 'One should not dwell in the specialness of the extraordinary experience',[20] he wrote and the thought was playing with me as I cycled down to the quarry. I did not really wish to experience my natural backyard like this. I did not wish for the iconic or the grandstanding. The peregrine, through no fault of its own, through its simple magnificence, took on in my mind the sheen of wildlife through a television screen. This was nature packaged and exaggerated. This was the natural world removed and made special, made separate and I would be merely the voyeur, enjoying a show that was forever removed from me. 'Everywhere, cameras effected disorientating changes of focus and speed, regardless of appropriateness, so that pictures lost touch with authentic sense experiences',[21] Richard Mabey wrote of a gloomy time spent watching television wildlife programmes and waiting now to see the extraordinary I felt something of that distance. I recalled growing up in the city and on how looking out of my box-bedroom window I had once seen the sudden appearance of a small flock of goldfinch feeding on some overgrown thistles. They were the most exotic wild birds I had ever seen, like miniature Japanese paintings. I can still see them now, swaying at the head of the plants, across the boundaries of the council-installed, half-collapsed picket fence. They were unusually beautiful but their appearance in that backyard, there amongst the paving slabs and the washing lines, the sheer ordinariness of their feeding on those thistles, gave me a full sense of attachment. Sure, I was here by the quarry in person, I was following the simple advice, 'that's the way to see the world: in our own bodies',[22] but I was struggling against that feeling of remove. I was ambivalent.

I was wrong. Or at least I am nearly convinced I was wrong. While waiting by a stand of gorse I lifted the optics and there was the peregrine on a ledge. The colouring was deep and strong. I could see the dark bars of the lower body, the yellow toes, the terrible alertness of the face. I thought again of how, directly through human activities, a species found on every continent had faced worldwide extinction. I could see clearly that this was a marvellous bird. I thought also that to write of it would be a little like writing of an eagle soaring or a whale breaching the water, that words would indeed be superfluous. As I watched it some crows flew around it, a pair of pigeons passed over the quarry, almost as if all involved recognised that the peregrine was not, for this moment, a threat. I wondered had long residency made them all used to each other but I could not help feeling that the peregrine's tumultuous past and the evidence of this quarry as having once been a working place made the bird's tenure here unlikely to have been a venerable one. Looking up at the sheer face of the rock I thought of the County Waterford landowner and naturalist, Richard Ussher, the principal author of *Birds of Ireland* published in 1900, who was said, amongst the exhaustive work he carried out in producing his book, to have 'climbed the most dangerous cliffs, swam out to islands, and relentlessly pursued the peregrine falcon'.[23] Standing in the cool air I found that kind of dedication heartening and uplifting. I thought of how those singular moments from the past now survived as gifts to the present. Richard Ussher and many others like him still deepen our understanding and attachment today. Even in the 1980s a study of Ireland's choughs referred to Ussher's work of nearly a century before, his climbing and diving and insistence, and found that many of the same nest sites were still occupied. Between the peregrine crouched on the rock ledge and myself, lie all of those other observers and observed, the peregrines Ussher found, the choughs he counted. There is, I thought again, always company. From a lost oral tradition through to the monks and their nature poetry, Giraldus and Roderic O'Flaherty, Ellen Hutchins and Richard Ussher, there is a sense of continuity. A sense, perhaps, even of that most elusive quality, a sense of home.

Ussher's peregrine is 'resident and frequent',[24] its pesticide slump having not yet occurred and indeed he goes as far as pointing out that owing to its habits it was not as susceptible to poisoning as the eagles, much of whose demise in Ireland had followed on the eating of contaminated meat. I think, too, as I watch the still-resting bird on the ledge, of how Ussher wrote of the peregrine's hereditary attachment to its eyrie and of how a 'remarkable instance is that of High Island, off Connemara, still inhabited by these birds, where O'Flaherty wrote in 1684 that "yearlie an ayrie of Hawkes is found"'.[25] Are they still there? Could these birds I watch now, could they after all be descendents of birds that were here in 1684? The ravens, the choughs, the swallows so far away, all these geographically faithful birds, is there a genetic link between them all and these few miles that I explore? Do I watch the descendents of birds O'Flaherty saw and Ussher sought out and detailed? Ussher writes, too, of the peregrines and says that 'along the coasts and islands of Cork and Kerry a long chain of eyries may be traced, one on each precipitous island'.[26] The headland where I sat and missed the last of the swallows and saw the joyful choughs, had peregrines nested there? On the little headland maybe, by the inaccessible fortress? Where I watched the gannet diving 400 years after O'Flaherty had stood somewhere else along the Irish coast and watched gannets too? There?

However beguiling the notion is and however true it may well be for other species, the reality for the peregrine is almost certainly different. By 1986, after the worst excesses of the pesticides about which Carson wrote, it was being noted of the peregrine falcon that whilst recovery had taken place 'the coast remained relatively untenanted'.[27] The worked quarry and the years of absence all make this peregrine I watch most unlikely to be one of a link that has been here for centuries. In the cold winter sunshine, ignored by jackdaws and doves, the peregrine is a returnee, a survivor.

I cycle away alone through yellow clouds of defiant gorse. I have watched the peregrines through a relationship between people and birds that is surely as long as sentient man. I have heard the voices of those who watched the world before me and been lucky enough to read some of their words. I have seen the fields where absent birds once were. I left the fireside to see the highly valued, to see one of those the cameras might fix upon and I tried to see beyond that and I am not sure I fully succeeded. As I cycle back along the cold lane though I think of the peregrine there on its sheer, bare ledge. I think of it sitting unmoving for the whole time I watched. I think of its otherness and its undeniable beauty. And at night back by the fire I think of it out there along the coastal cliffs, hunting along the estuary and the fields and I think of the incredible speed it attains as it swoops on its prey, the whole magnificent indifference of the raptors. I think of what happened to the peregrine across the world and how it disappeared here in Ireland too, of how Ireland once had as many as fourteen resident species of birds of prey, eleven even as late as the 1800s and of how this was only five a mere hundred years later. I think of all that persecution and all that poisoning. Of how the peregrine remained 'only by holding on in the remotest corners of the country'.[28] I sit by the fire thinking on all that and think of that returned bird above the disused quarry, and the winter's night is suddenly warm and full of hope.

Birdsong may have had something to do with the way humans acquired language.[1]

J. Aitchison

6

The Backyard and the Song

The way I come back from the peregrine brings me over a stone bridge. It spans a not particularly broad but nonetheless fast-flowing river. The old bridge is curved by two wide arches and I halt a little while to lean over it and then walk down to the river's edge and stand and watch the quickly passing water. In Ireland rain is never too far away and these gathering winter days have often been wet. The river is high. I walk a small way further on as the air itself seems to move with dampness and I take shelter beneath the arches themselves. There as I watch the water breaking over boulders and rocks I notice on the other side a dipper bobbing up and down on a stone. Somehow, I feel as if I am seeing the bird in a far more fitting habitat than when I saw it not so long ago beside the morning traffic of the town and this bird seems to possess, too, more of the vitality and energy normally associated with it. This time I am fortunate enough to see it disappear under the free moving water and walk beneath the surface. It is dipping. This is a small memorable feat, this little movement, something in itself. As I watch it beneath the moss-damp arches, though, it is the shallow water beside the supermarket that somehow comes to mind. For all of the completeness of seeing it here, the beauty of it, to my surprise it is the memory beside the traffic and the building site that is more invigorating, more cheering. It is as if, no matter what we do, nature comes to us. It does not give up.

I recall, as its plump body comes back on to the stone, that the white-banded dipper has, on account of its shape, been referred to as a 'giant, dark, barrel-chested wren',[2] and while it certainly fits that picture it is another comparison which comes, on this occasion, more readily to mind. Records suggest that in parts of Ireland the dipper is still sometimes known as the 'water blackbird'[3] and in these winter days, whether beneath this dripping bridge, or beside the supermarket, it is the noise of birds like the blackbird that I miss most, whose absence, I think, is felt most keenly. These days are not just grey and damp, they are often, the unending crows besides, silent.

The American poet Gary Snyder has written in some detail about the idea of sacred places. He moves through the notion of what is sacred and what, by contrast, is not. He opens up the grasp of it, taking the sacred out of confinement. 'The land itself was their chapel and their shrines were hills and creeks and their religious relics were animals, plants, and birds.'[4] I am distracted by this idea during these quiet, winter days. The rain falls steadily outside the window and the whole of the island seems in retreat. In truth, the kind of worship Snyder quotes was in Ireland, in common with most modern, western countries, long ago forced into abeyance. The Catholic Church struggled its way around the pagan licentiousness that often accompanied holy wells and pattern days but essentially the sacred was withdrawn into the institution. The missing song of the blackbird, though, has me thinking of where the sacred might be, has me recalling how the birdsong of an evening, above a concrete yard, makes me feel. It is the sound of another season. To touch the sacred, in these days of rain and absence, I will have to experience something that is in many ways a contrast to the song. I know, though, that at least I need only walk, follow the map, the directions from the farmer on the lane. I will set off when the rain abates. I will find the sacred lying bare in the Irish countryside, for not far from here, a walk of an hour or so, there is a Mass rock.

I decide that the only way to truly visit the Mass rock is to do so as all of those who used it would have: on foot. You cannot make a pilgrimage by car. I am back at the beginning again. 'Walking is the great adventure, the first meditation, a practice of heartiness and soul primary to humankind.'[5] The 'turbulent democracy of little hills'[6] awaits me, the spilt evidence of human activity, the roads shooting off in every direction. Within them is the Mass rock.

We cannot know all of the hidden corners of the land that have been held in special reverence. We do not know, by definition, all of the intangibles, the places filled only with thought, that have been lost. We can only imagine them. The spectacular vistas we judge have been seen before. The majestic tree. The vanished, soaring eagles above an Irish forest or coast. The standing stones and the passage tombs we stand in awe of. Some of these we still possess. The Mass rocks, more humbly perhaps, signifiers as they were of powerlessness and poverty, are part of this, too.

Possessing a strangely low profile, Mass rocks can be found throughout the Irish countryside. They are hard, material, evidence of a harsh time, when Ireland under the Penal Laws saw the celebration and practice of the majority

Catholic faith prohibited. Still, whatever contradiction this entails, Mass rocks appear to have something insignificant about them, something that almost takes them into the realm of folklore. Over the last decades there has been a concerted challenge to the assumptions of Irish history, a redressing of the conventions. It is now suggested that the penal days were not as severe as was once thought, the amount of Catholic Irish that kept land and even went on to make money, is proof of history's inherent anomalies. As signposts to the ever elusive truth these points are necessary and well worth making. Mass rocks, though, inhabit a different sphere. These slabs of countryside, often marked by a neglected, faded signpost, come from that different corner, that narrative of the ordinary, that is so often overlooked. Mass rocks have survived, by and large, simply through a folk memory of where they were.

I walk the long straight road initially and follow it this time to the next village, a small settlement where the one pub-cum-shop closed at the same time as a row of new houses was built. There is still a church and a school. I go straight through the village, which is quiet and empty at this time, quiet and empty most of the time. The road begins to curve up and I can see the land around me begin to open. I am in the middle of a gentle-sided valley, though in truth, one or two of these roads are steep. At the top of some of them are long, wide views. My path now is off to the right, a narrow roadway with grass growing down the middle. The first house I pass is an old farmhouse with worn, heavy trees and some outbuildings that appear to disappear into a copse at the back of the house. All is quiet. Soon there is a smattering of newer houses, large and often severe looking. The ground around them is bare and clipped with straight, dead walls. There is another road now off to the left and it is along here that the Mass rock lies. There is a low stone bridge just above the level of the road and shallow water tumbles over stones beneath it. There are trees and the outline of overgrown hedgerow. On the right, partially obscured by branches, is an old white signpost for the Mass rock. Opposite it there is a large commemorative stone to those who died and emigrated during the Great Famine. I stand for a while on the quiet road. I wonder, with its mixture of running water and Mass rock and Famine commemoration, if this spot is actually a place long associated with beliefs and lore, with a rich and varied set of beliefs that pre-dated, lived alongside and was then assimilated by the Irish Christianity of the countryside. Could that in fact be why it was chosen as a place for Mass? Mass was held in these places against the edicts of the authorities when the Catholic establishment had lost its churches and lost most of its priests. By word of mouth the message would go around the countryside, along these lanes and hills I have walked, that Mass would be held on such and such a date at this particular place. A crowd would gather from across the fields. Lookouts would be posted to watch out for any approaching authorities. A Mass would be said and the rock was the altar. Here in a place that may well have been held as special, as apart, as sacred for a long, long time.

There are steps going around the bottom of a field and these then drop sharply, damply, down to the fast, noisy, shallow bed of water. There is a large flat rock here leaning out over the stream and on it there is a large cross. Would mass have been said here, by the sound of the water and within the trees? Would that have hidden the congregation well, kept them secret? Where did the lookouts go? Did the water noise and the obscuring trees not endanger them all? Though now that I look more closely I see that none of these trees appears old. Was the landscape different then, barer? Were there long fine views across the fields? I slip as I go down to the water's edge, a wet, mossy stone upending me. The water runs and on each side I am sheltered by steep escarpments of rock and earth. There is a natural secrecy here. The land hides you.

I stand and observe the length of the water both ways. I look up at the stone above me. Snyder would tell me, I think, that the Mass rock is not sacred because of the Christianity that went on here, nor is it sacred despite it. It is not sacred because of the other beliefs that may well have been associated with it. It is simply sacred because of them all. It is sacred because of the people who gathered here, because of the considerations they had when they were here. 'Sacred refers to that which helps take us out of our little selves into the whole mountains-and-rivers mandala universe. Inspiration, exaltation, and insight do not end when one steps outside the doors of the church'.[7] It is a special place because we know that there was a form of reverence here, at least once, and all these years later, knowing that, we can stand in this spot too.

On the way back up the steps I notice, beyond a growth of bush and briar, that there is the ubiquitous dump: bags of old refuse, furniture, a television. It is shameful. It makes me stop and look. The water continues and the wind picks its way through the trees. Perhaps this special spot is not so special after all. The dumping diminishes it. Or perhaps the sacred may remain, whatever the setting; 'all the land about us, agricultural, suburban, urban, as part of the same territory, never totally ruined, never completely unnatural'.[8] Something essential, something of the land itself might still just be. A city street with an owl calling. A small, beaten, urban garden where a goldfinch feeds. A house sparrow on a washing line. The sacred, the mystery of it, is not dependent upon scenery. Nature, again, does not give up. I linger again to think this through, to see if the sacred stays, but I linger out of sight of the dump.

As I come away from the Mass rock, having stood a while in the shelter of the running water, I think of how little mention there was of these sites amongst the different texts I looked at before coming here. I wanted to carry the content of the place, the knowledge of it, in my mind as much as possible but did not really find anything. Admittedly, I did not carry out an exhaustive, academic study of all references and examinations of the Mass rock in Ireland but having done a general snoop around, a root through texts that had stood me in good stead for most of the other things the land has been revealing to me, I found on this occasion a surprising reticence. I found an insignificance. So, as I walked back along the lanes, my pace speeding up as the cold gathered around me, my thoughts ran once more to the standing of these landscape phenomena. I know there will be references to them, there will be devotional works about them or particular studies that refer to the past with righteousness or simplification. In the general study, though, there seems to be very little and as I have not come here for a defined devotional reason or for the reassurance of an over-simplified past, I cannot but note the emptiness. It is as if the Mass rocks are lost to intellectual respectability, trapped somewhere between a narrow, one-tone narrative of history, the doctrines of a particular Christian creed, or the disregard of a newer, more elaborate version of the past. Which, as I walk away, is a gap, a missing page in the manuscript of landscape around me. For in essence I cannot help feeling that the Mass rock I have just left is part of what Seamus Heaney called our 'common emotional ground of memory and belonging'.[9] It is part of the consciousness that comes with walking these lanes and climbing into these fields. In many ways, too, it is one of the most powerful, as it is quite simply a piece of stone. If it really is the case that 'the struggle of man against power is the struggle of memory against forgetting'[10] it is of no consequence what the power is or what version of the past it proffers. It is only the remembering that counts.

The old farmhouse at the top of the gorse-lined lane that I return to has, as I have mentioned, a few old outbuildings around a concrete yard. In the spring and summer the outhouses are alive with nesting birds, but at this time of year they are silent. They are low and solid and though they leak and are mildewed, have doors and windows missing in parts, the general feeling you would get from them is that they will stand, in all their unadorned simplicity, for a long time to come. They are faded and utilitarian but their decline almost seems to be part of them. There is nothing remiss about it. Like a weathered tree they have experienced the years and the seasons. The concrete yard that surrounds them was obviously some later improvement to counteract the mud of wet, mucky ground. In parts of it there are the old prints of long-gone hens. Yet I truly believe that this plain yard, somewhat shabby even, is at times a sacred place. I went to the Mass rock to see one aspect of sacredness but I knew all along that it was here too, for the thing that first sent me thinking on such things occurs here in spring and summer, when the silence of the winter is replaced. This concrete yard outside my backdoor becomes sacred when the blackbird sings.

Some 6 million pairs of blackbirds are thought to exist between here and our neighbouring island, Britain. It is the finest example there could be of how the commonplace can still be beautiful. The contrast with peregrine numbers, or choughs, or grey partridge or the almost vanished corncrake could not be greater. The specialness of appearance and song, though, is unaffected. Still, even here, amongst the everyday, the bird of the suburban lawn as much as the old country hedgerow, knowledge can be misplaced. I had always thought, had always believed I'd read, that blackbirds were originally birds of the clearing, that they had flourished as farming had advanced, as their natural home in the glades had spread. This would have accounted for how they thrived amongst the manicured lawns and the shrubberies. The songbird came out into the light and has sung ever since. In this way the clearing of Ireland's forests would have spread the numbers of blackbird. The retreat of the trees would have been its advance. The spread of man would have been heralded by its song. Looking at those figures, the population in the millions, this would make perfect sense.

This, however, is wrong. It seems this was not the case at all: 'Studies of populations in Poland's Bialowieza Forest, some of Europe's last primeval woodland, indicate that blackbirds were originally birds of the high tops, their dark coloration and low-frequency song having strong parallels among canopy-dwelling thrush species of tropical rainforest.'[11] The blackbird, originally a resident of the interior of the forest, a songster at the top of those vanished wildwoods, did not find its natural home mirrored in the suburbs and the hedge. It adapted. The blackbird marched along with man even though it was originally at home amongst the dark, interior canopy of the forest. When the trees held sway that song rang out from treetop to treetop, not at the edge of the glade. When the forests were there, that song rang out at the very top.

Imagine for a moment that a monk is sitting in the open,

working. He is transcribing a manuscript. It is sometime in the ninth century. It is summertime and it is a dry day, perhaps even sunny. He glances up and breaks for a moment from his work. He is distracted. He hears something and maybe even has it in his view. He sits for a while, thinking. He scribbles what he thinks in the margin of the manuscript and all these years on we can still see what he wrote, hear what he heard. 'A wall of forest looms above/and sweetly the blackbird sings/all the birds make melody/over me and my books and things.'[12] The wall of forest? Is the monk still seeing the bird of the high tops, the dweller of the wildwood? Whatever the case, when we consider the words of all the others who looked out over an Irish landscape, the blackbird is everywhere. Other voices from these early centuries, often scribbled too in the margins of some manuscript, linger with the blackbird. 'Ah. Blackbird, it's well for you/whatever bush holds your nest/little hermit who clinks no bell/your clear, sweet song brings rest,' says one.[13] 'The whistle/of the bright/yellow billed/little bird./Over the loch/upon a golden/whin a blackbird/stirred,[14] says another. Perhaps it is the simplicity of these poems, the short, terseness of their observation that means the immediacy of the bird still seems within them. Is still there for us now. We can look at a blackbird and see what the scribbling monk saw when he looked. 'Stop, stop and listen for the bough top/Is whistling and the sun is brighter'[15] is 'The Blackbird of Derrycairn' and in the fourteenth century someone is calling out 'Your blackbirds and thrushes/an amulet against loneliness'.[16] Down through all these Irish centuries the blackbird's song is sounding. 'Nowhere on earth have I heard/a lovelier music than yours.'[17] Or back again to one more monastic scribe, breaking from his labour sometime in the ninth century, 'A bird is calling from the willow/with lovely beak, a clean

call./Sweet yellow tip; he is black and strong./It is doing a
dance, the blackbird's song'.[18] It is doing a dance, a monk
wrote in the ninth century in Ireland of the blackbird's song,
and the blackbird's song is still doing a dance for us now.

There is a well-known story about St Kevin of
Glendalough and a blackbird. In this tradition St Kevin was
praying and had his hand held out to heaven in praise and
supplication. A blackbird, as Kevin prayed, chose his
outstretched hand as her nesting site. For fear of moving and
disturbing the bird St Kevin waited until the eggs were laid
and the young hatched before shifting his hand. There is
nothing like Glendalough here in this concrete yard, nothing
approaching the sanctity and beauty of that place. There is no
St Kevin standing in the yard unwilling to disturb God's
creation. Yet, looking out at the concrete on my return,
feeling the colourless weight of winter and the silent skies
that only swish with rain, I know that this yard too can be a
sacred place, however exaggerated that might seem. This
yard, too, becomes like a place of worship.

In springtime, as the swallows return and the trees green,
the blackbird sings. Sometimes it is on top of the old ash,
which has many of its branches torn and missing from a
winter storm, like amputated limbs. From a high branch, like
its forest-dwelling ancestors, the blackbird's sound carries.
There is usually an answering one from somewhere across
the fields. One wet spring evening last year, when the light
had retreated again and the just-returned swallows had
disappeared once more above the low clouds, the dusk,
briefly, brought sinking sunshine. I stood in the yard and
heard in the distance the droning, dreary, swish of traffic on
the main road. Then the blackbird began to sing. The damp
ground and the dripping trees no longer mattered. The threat
of the road receded. The blackbird sang as if singing were the

only reason to be alive. I stood at the end of a damp, cheerless day and the oblivious song was all that mattered. There could have been no other response, no other fitting response, than to stand and listen. The concrete yard, the mildewed outhouses and their leaking roofs, the nearby pollution of the main Cork road, it was all for that moment sacred. The salvage of the song, why could it not make of the yard a sacred grove? 'Great Brown Bear is walking with us, Salmon swimming upstream with us, as we stroll a city street'.[19] Blackbird, too, is singing for us, as we sit in a suburban lounge, lie in a hospital bed, or stand in a concrete yard.

And, like the peregrine, words seem inadequate in describing the blackbird's song. Vocabulary does not seem appropriate. Language would just get in the way. Which, as I think back on all those voices, those scribbled handwritten notes in the margins of a vellum manuscript, I see those earlier observers had long ago realised. They had thought this long before the thought came here, to this wet yard. The simplicity of their words, the unadorned descriptions they offer, that is the only true acknowledgement. 'A hedge before me, one behind,/a blackbird sings from that,'[20] someone wrote early in the ninth century. A blackbird sings from that. Nothing else needs to be said. Let the bird sing. As the poet Francis Ledwidge did many Irish years later, before leaving his hillside village of Slane, to die amongst the wasted mud of Ypres in 1917. 'The Blackbird blows his yellow flute so strong,/And rolls away the notes in careless glee.'[21] All of those centuries later the song remained the same and remains the same now. The only thing to do is listen.

I set out because the silence of winter days lay heavy and the song I thought of and missed led my mind down certain paths, to a Mass rock and the notion of the sacred. I found a short distance away a place of celebration beside water and stone and trees. A place of defiance and resistance, a place where the powerless gathered. I found a dump of modern refuse and turned my back on it, a little defeated. Yet, back in the yard I had brought enough of the sacred with me to get closer, amongst the cold concrete, to the song and all those before me who had stood on this small island and celebrated it. There was enough passed down to me, enough simple truth, for me to hear again the immediacy of what the winter hid away. I went inside and knew the song would come again and knew that somewhere, even when we extend ourselves into the extraordinary, into discussing the sacred, that gifted voices still speak to us with simplicity and clarity. 'On the grass when I arrive,/Filling the stillness with life,/But ready to scare off/At the very first wrong move./In the ivy when I leave./It's you, blackbird, I love.'[22] It's you, blackbird, I love. And I am back, again, at the beginning.

*By the blue heaven, by the rolling sun
bursting through untrodden space, a new
ocean of ether every day unveiled.*[1]

Richard Jeffries

The Unsophisticated Spot

On the cold morning that I see the otter I am out and about on the streets of the town very early. It is the time of the delivering bread van or the returning, weary night worker. On this morning, waking up as I walk along, I realise that I am walking through a country made of water. Throughout the night rain had fallen. From inside the safety of the house I had judged it as falling in steady, relentless amounts. This was no storm, as often blows in from the Atlantic, loose and unruly. This was ordered, complete rain. It fell and it fell. Then, as the light broke through and the grey half-light leaked into the house, it stopped. Now, the heavy clouds lie on top of each other across the sky, jostling the morning into smallness. There was dryness in this sky at dawn but the water was already everywhere. Sudden ponds had appeared in the fields, streams had become rivers and rivers had become lakes. Channels of rushing, shallow, gravel-filled water ran along the roads. The clouds above were grey and spent. The land below was water and motion. The rain had fallen and now that it had stopped

I was drawn to what it had left behind.

'The lakes, rivers, marshes, fens, bogs and, in coastal areas, estuaries, saltmarshes and lagoons were so vast and untamed . . . It is difficult nowadays to envisage how much greater they were in extent compared to the present.'[2] This description of an Ireland at the start of the seventeenth century is, on this morning at least, not so difficult to imagine. After the night's rain it is easy to see how wet Ireland is, to wonder as I walk along whether this heavy rainfall is as it was in past centuries and if so, with so much wetland now drained, where it all goes. This morning it has come out on to the footpath, has leaked across the road, is running from every rooftop and through every gutter. Some thirty years ago, on the edge of the city, I remember acres of black, watery bogs. There was low tree cover and there were little-used paths. There was an air of neglect and disuse that segued into a feeling of wilderness and nature, right there on the urban fringe, minutes from the corporation housing estates, just beyond the gull-rich fields of the city dump. I cannot find that land now. The housing estates are around every corner. A shining, surface efficiency has replaced the air of disuse. The new country lives here. The dump is still there, even if it is closing down, but even that can no longer orientate me. Roads have been built and cars now rush past and the shape of the city has changed. I see at least some part of a golf course where I think the bogs were but it is gone from me now. Perhaps that is as much to do with there being less licence to roam than there was, or simply less opportunity for an adult to do so than a child. It is highly unlikely however, I think as I look over to where that wetland used to be, that it remains. It has surely been drained and the black lakes within it gone, and the stand of trees and the mysterious hut in the reed beds where we imagined a hermit lived, knocked down. What rich life was in those reed beds and those deep black waters, those wetland trees and that boggy land, I do not know. We never saw any other people there, we never saw any signs of development. The paths to it now have gone and I suspect it no longer exists.

On the deserted, wet streets, an entirely different Ireland comes to mind. This one is less obvious, even somewhat peculiar but I think it is the regenerating freshness of a land suddenly dominated by water that brings it to mind, the feeling of a landscape created anew. Again it is an Ireland I cannot imagine but at the end of the last glaciation the Irish landscape waited to become itself. It was a blank canvas. 'The landscape then was a clean slate almost devoid of plants . . . As the ice retreated from Ireland, the new landscape, re-modelled by the ice, was revealed.'[3] What lies before me on this wet morning is nothing like that, it is not a tundra-like scene awaiting the colonisation of plants, it is not grey-soiled or in any way barren. It is wet and green. It teems with movement and does not have the stillness of a land the ice has only just left. It is not even the water of the melting ice or the idea that 'rivers flowed under the ice taking melt-water to the ice sheet margin'[4] that brings that forgotten landscape to mind. It is instead the idea of the newness of it all, the thought of a land only just coming into being. For at this moment, on this morning, walking the deserted roads into the quiet streets of the town it is as if time is just beginning in a land dominated by the element of water. Indeed, there is little other sound than that of the water, water running and moving across the fields and the tarmac and the concrete in ways I cannot judge. I am aware as I walk along that this new land has me at its mercy. I would not be well equipped to move through a land ruled by wetness and sudden streams and broad rivers. Even as I reach the streets of the town this feeling of a land created anew remains. There is no one about and no traffic has yet begun. It is just the water.

The sight of the otter, then, is really very apt. I am in the otter's habitat, the otter's wet world, even though I stand on a concrete bridge, just off yet another bypass. But all of that is quiet and although the lights in the garage are beginning to wink when my walk takes me to the bridge to look at the now swollen, moving, restless river, the new estate sitting precariously close by, the appearance of the otter is simply a confirmation. For on this morning this is a wet, aquatic world and on this morning this is a land where the otter excels.

Ireland's otters, though part of the sad, general decline that seems to characterise so much of the natural world, constitute a very important percentage of the European population. The otter is starkly extinct in some of its former range. In comparison to a lot of our nearest neighbours, our otter numbers are very healthy. Like so many other things our otters, too, are distinctively Irish. Looking again to our nearest neighbour, Irish otters are noticeably darker than those in Britain. So what we have is a truly indigenous subspecies of the arctic otter, one resident here long enough and isolated long enough to develop its own characteristics. Interestingly, the archaeological evidence does not match this genetic suggestion of long residency on the island. According to that historical source the otter was not present until the Bronze Age. Reassuringly, this is far more likely to pinpoint the frayed limits of our knowledge than any actual discrepancy. As Michael Viney points out, the otter is 'well-capable of swimming across the North Channel of the Irish Sea. The absence of any earlier otter record may simply reflect the inadequacy of current archaeological evidence.'[5] Once again the natural world, the school where we can learn so much, reminds us of the limits of human knowledge, reminds us of the comforting randomness of living.

From the bridge on the wet morning I watch the otter. The air is grey and heavy and the otter, being in the distance, is indistinct. There is, however, a clarity about it in the water that fixes it in my gaze. It is completely at one with this rolling, wet world I have suddenly found myself in. The river is, at times, moving very quickly and there is clearly a lot of water making its way across the land. The otter, however, sits back in the water and bobs with every liquid movement. As I watch, what I see is a complete marrying of environment and animal. The otter is the master of this morning, not I. There is a completeness. I watch both an enduring cohesion and a daily re-creation. The otter is both ancient and fresh. For a while the other world of human activity is oblivious to all of this but slowly cars begin to pass and the occasional passer-by crosses the bridge too. The bypass begins to make its noise. I must move on and as I do, looking back across the river, I feel that although the human day has begun and the otter still sits astride the water, the obliviousness remains.

Not too far from here somebody else haunted Ireland's damp, wet places and as I think of that dripping bridge and the watery, cold corners of that morning I find that her name comes to mind easily. When Ellen Hutchins died in 1815 she was not quite thirty years of age, yet in that short, retiring life marked by ill-health, she left a legacy as both an Irish artist and a botanist. Such was her work in the natural field that 'the remarkable achievements of her short life are recorded in the several plants bearing her name, including *Herberta hutchinsiae*, the beautiful hepatic or liverwort, *Jubula hutchinsiae*, the dark companion of the Killarney fern . . . The flowering plant genus *Hutchinsia* was named in her honour after she discovered a plant of this southern European genus growing wild on a cemetery wall in Bantry.'[6] Studying the mosses, liverworts, lichens and seaweeds around her Bantry Bay home Ellen Hutchins entered into a minute study of the usually disregarded, in a life that never saw her travel far from her birthplace in that very same area. Recording these often drab plants in intricate, artistic detail she wrote that 'collecting and examining plants is the greatest amusement of my very retired life'.[7] She wrote further about where this collecting took her on those occasions when she was well enough to set out from her Bantry home and visit her 'favourite spot by the rocky, woody side of a little waterfall particularly dear to me . . . I have spent many happy hours creeping among its rocks and never quitted it without regret. The troublesome little affairs of this world continually deprive one of the enjoyment of such pleasures.'[8] I have no knowledge of what Ellen Hutchins found on her small journeys out from her home apart from the scientific observations and details that she recorded. I have no idea what other insights she may have had in a life so scarred by ill-health and a life eventually so short. I can only guess, only imagine. Indeed, in many ways it is somewhat peculiar that standing on a bridge watching otters on a soaking wet morning should bring to mind a character I had come across as a minor detail in a book. Still, that has been the nature of this study, from field to book and back, always believing that in the miniature, the everyday, the easily neglected, the short journey out from the door of the house, the only journey Ellen Hutchins ever made, that I would unearth a wealth of knowledge. Michael Viney memorably writes about this from his home on the west coast of this small island, wondering aloud about his 'vocation of perpetual curiosity', asking of himself, 'where do I get all this stuff – botany, folklore, history, etymology? From books, obviously . . . At one level, it is a mere ransacking of indexes to other people's work, but it has also taught me, rather later in life than I would like, to go out and observe things for myself . . . I sometimes think that one square yard of our acre, looked at closely enough in all seasons and interpreted with all that science and poetry and art could bring to bear, would support a rapt lifetime of discovery.'[9]

Which is where I began and where I find myself again, with the company of centuries to the company of today, with books under my chin like Michael Viney and like him, though a good few steps behind, 'trotting after someone else'.[10] Like Ellen Hutchins too, like Michael Viney, like Patrick Kavanagh, I have put my faith in a small area of wandering. I am coming out from my door still hoping that these small places might yet constitute a lesson about everything.

I set out on another cold morning, a year or two before the time in the town, deliberately to see otters. I did not expect to see them and I would not have felt any particular disappointment if I had not seen them but over the years I had glimpsed them once or twice, far in the distance, swimming by the coast or running across a strand with that peculiar humped gait. I was aware that the chances of seeing them by the coast were thought to be noticeably higher and that in comparison to the sightings of them in other countries the sight of an otter would not be astonishingly rare. These places were within easy reach, a long walk or a bicycle ride, so I thought I might see more than a floating otter, back reclining on the waves, or the movements of one in the dark, in and out of the street lights of a town that cast sodium moons on the bay water, or the hurried departure of one from sand to sea. Even the realisation that this amount of sightings of an animal that the guidebooks for Ireland tell me is extremely elusive has been very lucky, I find the idea of departing one cold dawn, hoping to see them, enough to get me up.

When I leave the day is still winter-morning dark but before long as I cycle out along the road a dim light is breaking through. The roads are deserted, although in the distance I see the lights of one or two cars raking across the winding roads. The air is cold as it passes by me. As I near the coast there are the lonely lights of houses or streets shining out across the water and the air itself seems suddenly damper. When I near the lagoon and the causeway and the broad inlet that comes in from the sea I lean the bike against a ditch and walk on. There is a mist lying above the water and the sound of stirring birds. The smoky cloud that blankets the water gives the scene an almost mystical backdrop. I stand still for a moment. There is the noise of the sea further out in the bay, and the waking birds, but all is muffled as if the earth itself is yet to stir, as if the mist that, as I watch, moves with the recognisable qualities of smoke, was some kind of sleep surface. I move on across the causeway, past the waters on either side and the noise of my feet on the gravel is loud and alone. In this sleeping world I find it hard to believe that my clumsy movements have not alerted all living things.

Out beyond this bay, on the dividing high rock between two fine beaches, sits a new hotel. It looks out over a wide sweep of sea but does so, as seems to be the fashion, through a car park. Why the car park and the helicopter pad get the best of the view I do not quite understand. Before, a modest hotel had stood here, but this is a much grander affair, with accompanying apartments. Still called an island, this corner of the coast has long since ceased to be so and is now heavily developed, leaning and yearning towards exclusivity. Walking beneath that hotel now, glancing up at the busy car park, it would be hard to believe that this is the same place where in '1641, some 600 Irish were drowned . . . a rag-tag rebel force retreating from English and Scottish troops under Lord Forbes, and cut off by the tide'.[11] Somehow, I think, as I listen to the waves breaking heavily in the distance, that if I were to set off there now on this misty dawn I might well be able to envisage that scene. The night, the dawn even, beyond the lights of houses or street, brings the untrammelled past closer.

I walk on a bit further but being only able to guess the time I turn back towards the lagoon, thinking that early commuter cars might soon be passing, the new traffic of the new country. Soon enough an early white van passes by, its high-pitched brakes loud at the corner. Its flailing lights disappear. I walk through cold air, and the light, slowly, slowly begins to lift. The mist above the water, if I stand long enough, appears as if it is drifting, dancing, waltzing away. The water of the lagoon lies dotted with sleeping birds. They are unmoving across its surface though I hear noise coming from some of them now, ghostly, high-pitched half-whistles. I position myself by a signpost at the causeway end of the water and stand there in the cold dawn. By now, to be honest, I have forgotten all about otters. I am more enamoured with this cold morning itself and the feeling of newness that I cannot know I will feel a few years later on the wet bridge. I gaze out across the still water, the reed beds away to my right, the far-off roar of the sea to my left and it is for this moment a quiet world again, even a deserted one. This small lagoon and its emptiness. These small moments of life renewed, as if a single day could be a beginning. The poet Rainer Maria Rilke wrote about this far, far away from here, when he wrote of resolving to 'be always beginning: to be a beginner'.[12] A morning like this feels strangely as if the world is just beginning. This wintery morning is somehow, for me standing here beside the signpost, like an instant of creation. It is hard not to be caught up in that while watching the life of the lagoon, the mist dispersing slowly above the water, the birds gradually waking, the constructed, human world nowhere to be seen. For this moment.

I do not know if I saw them first or heard something. Perhaps I even sensed some movement at a level I cannot describe. Whatever the case, I turn to my left and from the slope of the causeway and from the thorn bushes growing roughly there, I see them. For a moment the two otters move along this small shore but almost immediately they are in the water with a smooth motion that has come and gone before I know it. I stand still and frozen by the signpost. I do not move. I do not know whether they are unaware of me or have judged that I am harmless but the scene takes place without me. As I watch they swim past. Across the lagoon and with the waking birds beyond them the two dark shapes swim the whole length of the water. I can make out their figures, the head and some end of the flat tail visible above the surface, the wake that spreads slowly out before them. The moment does not seem hurried in any way and the ease of the otters in this element is obvious. I can see as they swim why people here call them river dogs, for that head held above the water brings dogs instantly to mind. They swim through a mist that now rises above them. It appears to me like an ancient scene. The frozen morning water, the smoking air, the absence of machine-made noise, the lightening dark, the otters moving slowly through the water, heading towards sleep as night ends. If otters have been here, as they probably have, since the last glaciation, this scene I watch may have happened again and again for over 10,000 years. Most mornings, indeed, during that long, long time. Each fresh, new, beginning morning. They disappear into the reed beds and for a short time I watch the small wake of their movement coming back to me.

Otter numbers are usually assessed by surveying likely sites for droppings, or spraints, as observing them is too difficult. I have stood on this new, cold morning and watched two of them, one much larger and leading the way, perhaps the mother, swim past me and away. I wait a little longer until I realise that the grey light of winter has arrived for this day and that cars will now be moving in numbers along the roads. I step away from the lagoon and walk back to the bicycle in the ditch.

When Rainer Maria Rilke wrote about the art of writing poems he suggested that creativity must be accompanied by a returning to 'that first innocence'[13] and to the 'unsophisticated spot'[14] where poems first found him. The Ireland of the blank canvas, when the ice had just retreated, might have had that first innocence. The seventeenth-century Ireland of vast lakes and bogs, too, might well have been an unsophisticated spot. Ellen Hutchins spent her short life looking in unsophisticated spots: damp, neglected places. Michael Viney, likewise, wandering his corner of County Mayo, described his life as being a vocation of perpetual curiosity, something very close to the state of that first innocence. Between them all I somehow found the otter. The otter roaming the unsophisticated corners of our land, the wild, untended spots. The otter, each morning too, if we are lucky enough to see it, moving through a country of rediscovered innocence. The otter, here in Ireland, at its densest population numbers in western Europe. The otter, for whom most recorded deaths are as the result of being hit by cars. The otter, in the wild, wet places.

On the mornings that I saw the otter – the morning on

the bridge and the morning by the lagoon – I did not look at a different country. I looked at this small patch of Ireland, as I do each day. It was wet and the otter came out of the wild and swam past me into the wild again. But I was in that wild, too. I had, as Gary Snyder has argued, carried the wild with me. I was not apart from the otter. We were parallel. The otter's life moved parallel to mine, parallel beside me in the lagoon, parallel for the few moments we shared passing each other by. The hope must be that we make room for these parallel lives. That we do not move too far away from the unsophisticated spots, too far from the possibility of that first innocence. From the knowledge of it.

I am left with the otters I was lucky enough to see. Left with those mornings. Left with the 'palpable, lithe/Otter of memory/In the pool of the moment'.[15]

*For time is the essential ingredient; but in
the modern world there is no time.*[1]

Rachel Carson

8

No Beginning and No End

Water is never far away in Ireland. Lakes, rivers, bogs. The hidden and forgotten streams. The black pools. Most of all, I suppose, the rain. The rain that follows rain. And then there is, of course, the sea.

These rainy days by the fire, recalling the otter-rich, damp hours, it is almost possible to forget the sea. Water is so much a part of the island anyway that the ocean becomes unnecessary. It becomes remote in its otherness. It is somewhere way out there. Fields full of overnight lakes, sudden rivers, streams running down the street, the air itself wet. They are all at hand. There is no call for the sea.

On an island, however, that cannot be the case for long, however much water there is on the land. The rain tattooing against the windows is fresh in, across the fields and hills, from the Atlantic. The wind drives in behind it. If there is to be a storm, it is not the cold winds that come down from the north that are to be feared, but the south or southwesterly ones that come in from the sea. They are the ones that will cause damage. No Irish scribe sits through a storm now, as one did in the ninth century, writing, 'bitter the wind tonight,/combing the sea's hair white:/from the North, no need to fear/the proud sea-coursing warrior',[2] but a storm can still bring comfort and fear in equal measure. There is the winter comfort of the fire and a storm outside in the fields, or there is the fear of high winds and loose slates, the house stretching in a gale. So close to the sea, the promise of a storm is never too far away.

On these wet, blowy days that we have now there is a ferocity about the sea, a physicality, an animal element. Those fine, soft days, of gentle, wet air, of a skin-soaking drizzle, that characterise so much of our weather, occur throughout the year, in any season, but these days are different. These days are restless, turbulent. These days would see a sea of white, high against the rocks.

One other truth about an island, at least an island like this out in the Atlantic, is that the weather is interminably variable. Seasons come and go in a day. A morning's rain can mean an afternoon's sunshine. An afternoon's sunshine can mean an evening's gale. Then, after the restless storm come days of peace, of stillness. On these days, the days of quiet after the days of noise, the sea stretches away beyond a flat horizon. On these days it is hard to resist the call to go and watch it.

Writing at the beginning of the last century, from her headland home so close to here, Mary Carbery was drawn again and again to the sea. She would sit and watch the Atlantic whenever she got the chance. Realising that her life, as the woman of the big house, was a life of comfort, she worried over the well-being of her poverty-haunted neighbours. She attempted to understand their lives, the life and spirit of a place, a place she described as being an 'earthly paradise'. A place she was always a few steps short of belonging to. Somewhere out on the ocean, she had been told, there was an island called Moy Mell. 'By and by the moon will make a wide path between us and Moy Mell, the island of blessed spirits. Once in a thousand years the way is open for the souls of the dead to come home.'[3] At this time of year as I look out the moon is often above the house early, is part of the daytime sky. It is not, though, Moy Mell to which I expect to see a path. It is merely the ocean I wish to look upon, the uncaring expanse washing the edge of the land. I want to see the waves, the unheeding, relentless waves, waves that are part of the myth of the island itself. From Amergin arriving across a span of nine magical waves to claim ownership of the country to Cliodhna's Wave attributed to the coast not far from here and just down the way from where Mary Carbery looked out for Moy Mell. 'Cliodhna's Wave is called after a pre-Christian goddess of beauty, who eloped with a mortal and was reclaimed by a wave sent by her sea-god father: later she seems to have dwindled into a mermaid, drowned in Glandore harbour.'[4] That harbour is much changed now, the playground by and large of a wealthy elite who may or may not know that Moy Mell is out there or that the mermaid drowned in the bay. The waves, regardless, still come.

The waves still come for there is, perhaps like nowhere else, a consistency about the coast that resists the alterations wrought elsewhere. If forests have come and gone and, if vast, black bogs have emptied and vanished, if numerous animals and birds have lived and died away, gone from the island for good, the coast continues. The coast endures, for where the ocean is, is a different territory. A territory of which we see only the surface, the angry, raw, or placid epidermis. Out there, beyond the nine waves, seabirds, sea mammals and fish live lives at the borders of our understanding. Out there is another planet. Yet, the sea surrounds us. The ocean is the true border, the natural margin of our picture. Out beyond there are continental slopes and Atlantic currents. 'Dogger, Rockall, Malin, Irish Sea:/Green, swift upsurges, North Atlantic flux,/Conjured by that strong gale-warning voice/Collapse into a sibilant penumbra.'[5] The poet making a poem of the sea out of a poem of the sea. Malin Head, Shannon, Valentia, Fastnet. Out there are guillemots, razorbills, kittiwakes, gannets. Jester-coloured puffins, even. Storm petrels staying at sea for months and months on end, without ever touching land. Out there are porpoise, dolphin and whales. Out there are seals.

Back where the waves beat the land, however, is the edge of the picture. Here the margin, border and fringe complete the painting. Without the shade and the light, without the interpenetrating zones of that shade and light, the picture is incomplete. There is nothing to occupy the edge of the page. Without the coast the sketch of one small, parochial, corner of an island, the form of it, is unfinished.

For all of the great unknown character of what lies out beyond and beneath the sea, where the waves meet the land is a point where change takes on a geological slowness. Here is the consistency. Of course, the coast too, like any other stretch of the island, is not immune to man-made change. Whilst this island's climate has excluded any Mediterranean style of coastal development, palatial homes or industry are not unknown along the fringes of the Atlantic, or the Irish Sea. The heady rush of progress has found a foothold here too. Much of the coast, however, remains undisturbed. Much of it is as it was. That aside, even away from the muddy waters that surround the very word 'progress', the coast itself, the very nature of it, is on a scale that is far different from our own. By that I do not mean just the sheer height of a soaring cliff-side, the simple impressiveness of the landscape, the imposing composition of a wild coastline. That stands to itself. I mean instead that the essential durability of the coast, to the human eye at least, continues, on and on. It endures. It remains, year after year after year. Maybe there, strangely enough, there at the beaten edge, the first and last resting place for all those departing swallows, maybe there lies the essence of a natural fidelity. The fidelity of the earth itself. For all the shifting scenery of the sea, the cliffs will remain as they are. The only change will be of a kind we cannot perceive, the kind that happens with a geological pace. Any other change, change of a cataclysmic kind, is likely to change us too. 'A million years here at the cove, or ten million, or a hundred million, are as yesterday. Before the mountains were begotten and the world was brought forth, from everlasting to everlasting, the sea has clamoured on this shingle.'[6]

I go back to the headland. The headland where I missed the departing swallows but saw the playful choughs. A place I remember from childhood. The sea has drawn me along and I make my way out along a familiar road, down familiar lanes and past the familiar grotto. Already there is a sense here of things unchanged. These overgrown lanes and the constant irregularity of the fields. The blue-cloaked statue of Our Lady still looking out to sea. Suddenly, yet deliberately, without haste, a heron takes off from one of the nearby fields. 'Joanie-the-bogs' I have heard it called here and that tells how a bird so often seen standing in the water of a river also frequents what may appear like a stretch of grass. Something about the bird as it passes over is ancient, like a cave painting or a fossil. A pterodactyl in the sky. One time I recall disturbing a heron as I turned the bend in a river and it threw itself away and flew, dropping its prey as it did so. The eel slid across the bank and fell back into the water. In short, fluid moments the little scene was over.

I make my way past the banks of biting heather. As I tread over it, it bounces back behind me as if I had never passed, but a plant surviving here, where the soil is thin and the rock shows through and the ocean is so near, would have to be hardy and indeed the heather is so hardy that individual plants can live up to thirty or even forty years. That is a long time to spend on these wind-scoured, salt-washed edges. As I stand for a moment I see the water that runs down these rocks and escarpments, runs continually day after day through the body and over the roots of these plants. Perhaps that thirty- or forty-year lifespan is not so much after all, for if this squelching land beneath me could be classified as a patch of bog, time would take on another dimension completely. 'The history of modern bog vegetation is revealed by the structure of the bog. It is only the top 50 cm of a bog which is alive. The plants sit on the corpses of their ancestors going back as much as 10,000 years.'[7] Unlike other habitats the bog depends on its past being locked up beneath it, not recycled above it. Could I be standing on thousands and thousands of years of vegetation, I wonder, here at the edge of the island, where human activity has not been extensive. I could be looking here at a consistency, a fidelity, that goes back as far as human involvement with this land itself: here on this small stretch of rock and bog and water and heather, the continuous waves beating their steady rhythm in the background. Over this brief area, this fragment of ignored land, is it likely the centuries have changed much?

This wet path is always difficult to follow. In many ways there is no path. There is a rough way of some sort but most of it is actually a track made by the water running off the edge of cliff a bit further on. The waterfall that falls into the bay below. A footstep can soon end up in a boggy hole or back into heather.

If this were the summer I could look down into that small inlet, lean out across the rich grass of the bank that lies against the edge, peer down on the water and rocks below. There would be gulls flying around and on ledges of sheer stone grey, unlovely herring gull chicks would hug the earth as the water crashed below them. From an inaccessible ledge below, one nesting gull would rise from a nest of moving chicks, a nest that virtually leans out over the unsteady waves.

On this day, in a winter that may be fading but has been doing so with something of a kick, those chicks are in the sky if they have survived. Gulls effortlessly glide winds and updraughts, currents in the air only they can see or sense, feel against their bodies. It seems from down here as much like pleasure as I could judge pleasure to be. They soar out over rocks and waves. Hungry. Watching. Passing the day. Passing the time. Over those same peaks of rock, in the summer just gone, I watched a family of gannets flying by. Two adults and three juveniles in varying stages of immature plumage, younger than the four years that marks their completed appearance. None of them broke away, none of them stooped into that astonishing 60-mile-an-hour dive, disappeared up to 15 feet below the water, made a thump that could be heard on shore, even above the sound of waves. They passed on, their 6-foot wingspan, their trademark cruciform outline silhouetted against the sky. There exists between here and Britain two-thirds of the world's gannet population, mainly on vast, offshore colonies, concentrated around these two, geographically insignificant islands. The ones I watch passing in the sky have a togetherness about them as they disappear around a curve of coastal rock and a joint purpose that is unknown to me. Again I remember how long we have stood here and watched gannets above the sea.

A chough call sounds over the cliffs and I sense again their playfulness. The call is like the squeezing of a child's toy. The wind blows offshore and then turns around and blows in from the sea. White waves break against the rocks and the water stretches away and away, the hue of it darkening as it gets further out. The coast curves away on either side of me, with inlets and jagged edges snaking their way around the island. To my right a lighthouse marks one headland. To my left a lighthouse marks another, beyond the other headland where I saw the ravens and walked through the woodland. I have never seen a raven along this particular stretch, although this patch of coast would be no great effort for such a powerful bird. The American writer Peter Matthiessen has called the raven the 'great requiem bird of myth and legend'[8] but I cannot help wondering how much psychology or story is now attached to that huge bird. How much importance or relevance do we attach to the actual, physical, material world around us? How much do we invest it with the power of myth? How much credence do we give the raven any longer? John Clare's village nest is long gone and the raven, that for so long lived around man and was a central part of our daily narrative, now exists on the edges of the island only and on the edges of our consciousness too. It survives in the physically neglected corners and, as much, in the mentally neglected corners.

I make my way along the narrow coastal path, the jagged rocks and the sea below me. I walk beside the bramble-covered, rock-strewn fields, the rough, unused quarters. I notice and run my hand along the remnants of wall and building as I approach the narrow crossing to the headland, wondering when last a human hand touched this stone. Leaning to one side I can see the four or five levels of stone, an insignificant part of the tower that stood here in this inaccessible spot. The tower was over 40 feet high and I try to imagine that as I stand on the approach to it and see the remaining stones. Above it is the sky. I attempt to fix it in my eye, to build it in my imagination again, but I cannot. I walk down, across the narrow neck of adjoining land and then up onto the spongy rush of the headland. The grass lifts my footstep up and sucks it back down again at the same time. The wind is now blowing in from the sea and the air is wet. The winter cold, though, has eased even as the breeze picks up. I seek the shelter of a grassy hollow and lowering myself down I find that the wind vanishes and the rumble of the ocean becomes something distant. Suddenly there is a different quiet from the quiet of natural noise that is always to be found here. Now I hear the sounds of the earth around me through the filter of the rocks and the stones. 'The poetry of earth is never dead,'[9] the song of it, the rhythm of it, but for a moment now there is quiet within the quiet. I see the ocean framed between a broken line of rock and grass. I see too that someone else has been here before me. Scattered around the hummocks of these grasses are the messy remains of a kill. Feathers and small scraps of bone. Did a fox come across that narrow neck of land, a bird in its jaw? More likely a peregrine falcon swooped powerfully, broke the body on impact and dropped into the hollow here, out of sight and out of the wind. Long ago climbing over these fields and rocks as a boy I saw a kestrel hovering over this piece of land. It barely shivered in the air even with the sea wind blowing against it and I thought then of this headland as an island. As I climbed further on I remember nothing of the remains of a fortified tower or of the waves below. I only recall seeing the bird of prey, the same kind I could see at the top of my street growing up in the city, hanging still in the air over what my childhood mind decided was an abandoned island. These years later I remember that long-gone kestrel. Years after writing his poem and desperately unhappy here in Ireland, Gerard Manley Hopkins must have seen an Irish kestrel and remembered, too. 'High there, how he rung upon the rein of a wimpling wing/In his ecstasy! Then off, off forth on swing,/As a skate's heel sweeps smooth on a bow-bend: the hurl and gliding/Rebuffed the big wind. My heart in hiding/Stirred for a bird.'[10]

I do not stay too long on the windswept headland at this time of year. The kestrels and the gulls, the fox and the grass are well adapted to this place but I am not. I walk around the small outcrop first, glancing down at the dark waters below, the white wash beneath. I climb down then, tiring of the buffeting of the wind. I try to run my hand again along the stone remains of the fortress, hoping for a moment to be in the same place as those hands that put the stone there so long ago. I cannot reach. Time is beyond me. I move on down the narrow line and back on to the broader earth where this narrow connecting neck begins.

Standing here, between the headland and the mainland I can see down to the rocks and the water below. There is a small shingle shore there, often, I would imagine, covered by the sea. This small stretch of coastline is a mixture of vast boulders, of slabs and shingle. It is washed continuously by the sea. How quickly, I wonder, has the sea eroded the earth here? How much has been worn away in the last fifty years, how much in the last one hundred, two, three, a thousand? How quickly does the ferocious power of the waves wear away those smooth slabs and those jagged rocks? Or does this little coastline appear much as it did when I first saw the kestrel, when Ellen Hutchins searched similar coastlines not so far away, when Gerard Manley Hopkins turned his unhappy eyes to an Irish sky, when Roderic O'Flaherty watched the gannets? Has it looked like this to hundreds and hundreds of years of departing and returning swallows? Did this little stretch of coast look much as it does now when the tower stood? Would it not, after all, have sounded the same as it does now? Would it not have smelled the same? Did the winds not blow in the same way that they do now? Did the waves not beat in, again and again, as they do now? Did somebody from the tower stand here as I am doing and stare out on the same thing? Matthew Arnold, who taught Hopkins before he went to Ireland, wrote of waves so old they had been heard by Sophocles. 'Listen! You hear the grating roar/Of pebbles which the waves draw back, and fling,/At their return, up the high strand,/Begin, and cease, and then again begin,/With tremulous cadence slow, and bring/The eternal note of sadness in.'[11] I watch those waves now, watch the water breaking over rocks, watched the sea as Matthew Arnold did on the south coast of England. As Chet Raymo did around the coast from here, watching the sea clamouring on the shingle. And once more I am back at a beginning.

If I turn in to face the land, turn my back on the ocean, I see the hard rock that weathers this sea and those waves day after day after day. I see some of the crust of the earth, something of what lies underneath the surface that I each day walk upon. If the unchanging waves and the consistent shingle speak of an endurance through the years, these rocks speak of time in a way that is at the fringes of human understanding. In the rocks beneath our feet, in the hard coastal surface I see before me, lies the history of the earth itself. If our modern world can be characterised by an absence of time, by an absence of the sense of time, considerations of geological time dwarf the span of humanity in a way that words are not equipped to express. But then, how could they be? The oldest rock of Ireland, the oldest part of the Irish surface, just 5 miles off the Donegal coast on the small island of Inishtrahull, is dated at being 1.7 billion years of age. What can that possibly mean? Tectonic plates and shifting continents. An Ireland that originally took shape near the latitude of what is now southern Africa and moved, over millions of years, to its current position. Paleozoic and Mesozoic. The age of Precambrian and Cambrian. Old Red Sandstone, Carboniferous rock and limestone. 'About 250 million years ago, Ireland was in the northern hemisphere at about the latitude of Egypt today and had a desert climate.'[12] How can that be imagined? Or what of this about the creation of mountains by eruptions from the earth's core: 'Beginning about 65 million years ago, it continued for 15 million years.'[13] How are we to imagine something continuing for 15 million years? Standing in front of these wave-stained rocks, these enduring surfaces, the shingle and the water behind me, how are such time spans to be understood? Climbing down the old, slippery path to the sea's edge I had thought of finding a sense of durability, of continuity, of waves still falling where they had always fallen, of seeing what those who had stood here years before had seen, had smelt, had touched. I had thought of Matthew Arnold's Sophocles, Roderic O'Flaherty and Ellen Hutchins. I had thought of Chet Raymo looking out at the same sea and seeing the shingle of a million years. I had thought I might grasp some of that but find, looking at the earth's crust, that I cannot.

I linger on, however. I look back between the sea and the rocks, standing still a while longer. I realise that even this standing still is itself a gesture. Walt Whitman's declaration, written before technology's grip on time had tightened, comes strangely to mind. 'I loafe and invite my soul,/I lean

and loafe at my ease . . . observing a spear of summer grass.'[14]
The cold gathers around me and I am far from summer grass
but standing still is its own declaration. I feel not so much
defeated as bewildered by the tunnel of time opened by the
rocks, after I had thought of the waves and the shingle as
ceaseless. I have no real concept of those millions and
millions of years. They make the earth seem unfathomable.
They bring the enormity, the vastness of a cold universe here
to the shore. None of this is original, I know, but the sense
of strangeness is there all the same. Somehow though, as I
turn back to the thin climb up I find that limit of our
understanding, that border to our knowledge, to our epistemological knowing, fitting. Not in the comfort of
ignorance but in an acceptance of our nature. In an
acceptance of the earth. After all, if a stray, out-of-season
swallow blots our ledger, a million years can be forgiven for
doing so too. Frank Mitchell accepts that his exploration of
geological development is of a time with 'no vestige of a
beginning, no prospect of an end'.[15] Standing between the
waves and the rocks that inherent humility seems the only
fitting thing to feel.

*As to the seals themselves, no scientific
study can dissolve their mystery.*[1]

David Thomson

9

Native Fishermen

I did not go to the ocean only to see the waves and the water. To be confounded by the age of the rocks. I went there hoping to see a seal.

I know there are dolphins off the coast, and porpoises and whales. I have been lucky enough to see them. Seeing a fin whale surface above the water, the second largest animal to have ever existed, within sight of the green fields and tumbling lanes, was as close to a heightened religious experience as it was to nature observation. The smell of the animal. The way the motion of its huge body out of the water put the passing of time on a different scale. It was extraordinary in every sense. But what I wanted to see was a seal. In many ways the experience of seeing the whale, the sight of dolphins hurtling endlessly through the water, all of these felt like grandstand events. Not that they were not special, were not deeply memorable. They were. They stay in my mind. What I have always been more drawn to, however, what this book celebrates, is the power of the ordinary. It is what calls me. The wandering away from the back door and a few steps away finding a sense of wonder. Which in many ways, I suppose, makes the seal a peculiar choice. But not really. Not the more I think about it. Wandering these coastlines as a child, clambering over rocks, diving off jetties, casting a hook into breaking waves of mackerel, I never saw a dolphin or a whale and never thought I would. I saw seals, though.

So I go back to the headland again a few days later. I have often seen the bobbing head of a seal below there in the waters and I take that walk again without any persuasion. I will try this time not to be distracted by the immutability of the rocks or by the contrasting havoc of years that they represent but I will fail. The huge turmoil of geological and biological life is above and beyond the simple wonder of a seal in the water. It opens up a different vista. The idea of the earth forming, of the island taking shape, of biological life coalescing into something we might recognise, takes me back again to the idea of the pristine day, the notion of an environment in perfect symbiosis. The fresh slate. The Garden of Eden moment. The myth of the lost idyll. To engage with all that again would bring me once more into good company, to lost forests, to Cobbett's goldfinches, or to the teeming plains of Barry Lopez. Or, closer to home, to the Gaelic poets, to their failing culture and the loss of a golden age. 'I have lived in a lovely place,/and will see the like no more./Dear God, how unworthy now!/There's a text for one who can read it,'[2] writes one in the fifteenth century about the collapse of the bardic schools. Yet that idea of a vanished moment of natural perfection, of a pristine environmental equilibrium, of man's golden age, is as much a corner of the human imagination as it is a physical reality. Through those ideas of a perfect natural world that 'we have lost. We lament our own alienation and tell ourselves that once there was a time when all of humankind lived in their happy state.'[3] The history of this island lends itself to that, too, and for a long time a Gaelic culture embraced it. 'Gaelic Ireland always seemed to be dying, if not at the funeral of a lord, then on the deathbed of a poet, if not in the loss of native speakers to death or emigration, then in the sheer impoverishment of the words in the spoken language. The very tradition seemed to draw sustenance from the prospect of its own death.'[4] I do not wish to fall into that. I do not want to always filter my experience of the natural world through that sense of loss or that harkening back to a different, better time, whether that time be biologically true or imaginatively true. I can only deal with the world as it is now, as it is around me. I do not wish to believe that nature is in the past. Thinking on a past of vast forests, or untamed bogs and lagoons, of miles and miles of goldfinches, or life-rich plains, could get very close to a sentimental cul-de-sac. It could cloud out each and every vision. There is always the risk that the truth will get lost in it. Because there was, for every lament for the fallen Gaelic order, another truth. On reading an account of the Flight of the Earls in 1607 and of how a great cry and lament went up from the shore at their leaving, the writer Peadar O'Donnell said he laughed out loud. 'According to the folk memory of his people, the peasantry of Donegal and Derry stood on the shores of Lough Swilly and cheered as the boat moved away.'[5] I will forget the seductive possibilities of past absoluteness. I will forget the bewildering rocks and wait for the seal.

Not that sitting on the headland leaves me totally free of that element, for the book that I bring with me situates itself at a moment of loss, too. The author states of his travels in 1940s' Ireland that 'I came only just in time to hear the last remnants of a pre-Christian culture'.[6] On this occasion, however, it is impossible to feel any kind of discomfort or stale repetition, for this book is David Thomson's beautiful, peerless *The People of the Sea*, about the seal culture of Scotland and Ireland. Here, too, there is talk of a biologically richer past but again there is no sense of a distortion upon reading it, only the sense of authentic experience. 'In the old days, would you believe it, I have seen a hundred seals below there at the mouth of the cave gathered like children out of school. You will see one or two now in the moonlight if you wait and watch. One or two is the most you will see for there is nothing now the way it was the old times . . . the sea hasn't the shoals of herring in it, nor the mackerel, nor none of the creatures that were.'[7] No, reading this book of wisdom I can see I have begun to make mistakes. There was no psychological yearning, no Arcadian longing in those vast, vanished Irish forests, in Cobbett's goldfinches, in Rachel Carson's huge bonfires of poisoned birds, or in those American plains of 500 million slaughtered creatures. It was true. The questions that came to mind about our lessened biological life needed to be asked.

The seals I have seen off this coast have been, by and large, not the common seal but the grey seal. Of the two species of seal resident in Irish waters the common seal is now rarer than the grey. The heads I sometimes see poking above the water, those large, watchful eyes, the dog-like appearance, the human-like aura, the presence, are those of the larger grey. Disease, natural predators, scarcity of food perhaps, the activities of man, all these have reduced the numbers of the now misnamed common seal. So it is the grey I have seen out there on the waves. The seal is descended from an otter-like creature but, unlike the otter, which is a creature of the water and the damp, the seal is an animal of the ocean. It is still tied to the land, breeding and resting on shore, but it feeds at sea and its body is streamlined, designed and adapted to the sea. Even the reproductive organs and the mammary gland do not mar that water-designed shape. That body is completely at home in the sea, built for moving through the water. Like the sea birds that breed on land but spend their lives above and on the ocean the seal lives between the two but, unlike those birds, with the luxury of flight to take them away, the seals are inherently at home in the waves. They belong to the sea. Look out to the sea, the anonymous ninth century Irish poet tells us, 'at the noble ocean teeming,/the home of agile/shining seals:/it is swollen/to full flood!'[8] So I follow those instructions, those encouragements, from centuries ago. I sit and watch the sea as that Irish voice did so many hundreds of years ago.

It is often said that when Ireland starved between 1845 and 1849, the seas off the coast teemed with fish. Yet the population starved because of the potato blight. As a result of that people have talked of this island lacking a sea culture, of not having an affinity with the sea. When I hear that I think again of Patrick Duffy's 'elite narratives', for the stories of the coast, the lives of the poverty-stricken fishermen, any intrinsic account of the island's seaboards would give the lie to that. Fish, primarily in the form of herring, was a common food source, fished from the waters I now look out on. 'So common were herrings in the labourer's diet . . . the highest consumption of fish was in coastal counties, almost forming a complete circular fringe around the country.'[9] The people ate fish. The people looked out to the sea. They went out into the ocean in their boats. It is, though, the nature of that ocean and the nature of those boats that goes a large way to explaining why teeming seas did not save them from famine. It was not that they turned their backs on the waves. It was not that they were not in touch with the ocean.

A large part of the Irish coast, in the south-west, west and north-west, is perilous; there are cliffs, rocks, treacherous currents, sudden squalls, and, above all, the Atlantic swell, surging from America across thousands of miles of ocean. By the nineteenth century timber was short in Ireland; in the west, practically speaking, there was none, and fishing boats were small, the largest being 12 to 15 tons. The national boat of Ireland is the curragh, a frail craft, often of considerable length, made of wickerwork covered originally with stretched hides and latterly with tarred canvas . . . The curragh was not suitable for the use of nets in deep-sea fishing, and according to an expert writing at the time the fish off the west coast of Ireland lay many miles out at sea in forty fathoms of water. A vessel of at least fifty tons was needed, capable of going out for several days, laden with nets, to face the frightful swell of the Atlantic. If a gale blew from the east the nearest port of refuge was Halifax, in Nova Scotia. The curraghs and small fishing boats of the Irish were 'powerless' in these circumstances; and an inspector, reporting from Skibbereen, wrote that the failure of Irish fisheries was due to the want of boats suitable for deep-sea fishing, though this coast and the coast of Kerry abound with the finest fish in the world.[10]

Some twenty to thirty miles along the coast from here lie the waters mentioned in that inspector's report and outside the town mentioned in that report lies a famine pit, a site of mass burial. Some of those lying there must have looked out on these waters too and must have done so out of a desperation of which I have no inkling. Always there is company.

One story tells of a baby lost at sea by two fishermen who

returned three days later, after the wake, to find the baby on a rock ledge seemingly having being nursed by a seal. The baby grew up to be a fine swimmer. I gaze out at the gentle swell and the foam. I watch a gull soaring by and enjoy a sudden ray of sunshine, but it is David Thomson's book that I think on. This book is proof enough alone of the very real links between this island and the sea and in Thomson's work it is the seal that is the focus. He describes what can only be termed a culture of the seal richly existing along these coastlines.

The last time I saw one was just here, below where I sit, in a small channel between the outlying rocks of the headland and the high sides of the mainland. Coming back from the headland I had followed the path down and out of sight of the water. When the way took me up again I looked down on the head of a seal in the water. It was already observing me. The large dog face, the huge, dark eyes, the strange human air. Somewhere in the swell was the body, out of sight, perfectly placed beneath the waves. I stopped and watched and the seal stopped and watched. This felt like a shared curiosity. The seal disappeared in one fluid, silent, movement, the body fleetingly promising to appear at the surface, the water and the seal all the same element. I looked out at the water in between the rocks. A short distance away the seal resurfaced, observing me again. A moment later it surfaced in a different direction, some way back beyond where I had first seen it, its head buoyed above the water. Silence accompanied all this movement. I leant forward, wishing to move my sleeping legs, taking a step to the side. The seal was gone. I watched a while longer. A little further out it resurfaced. It stared over at me again. Then it was gone again. And then a little over to the right. Further out. Gone again. I had the sense of its undulating swimming movement, although I could not really see the body. Further out. Gone again. Surfacing again. Gone. The waves lifting up, coming in and in. The surface moving and moving. The restless peace of the sea. The seal gone.

I watch the ocean a while longer until the gulls pass over in numbers and the cold creeps up. Far over the hill I hear the childish call of the chough. I walk away with the waves at my back. David Thomson warns that seals have a 'dream-like effect on the human mind'.[11] He is, of course, right.

'But a lot o' those other stories is lies. We think it is lies, said Thomas. But it was true some time. It happened some time. All those things happened.'[12] In recording the incredible depository of folklore he found along the Atlantic seaboard of Ireland David Thomson has not only left us a wonderful book, he has left living proof of the rich, profound culture that this island shared with the sea. His work portrays a set of beliefs and stories that are nothing short of animist in nature. If it is hard to walk the lanes of Ireland without Robert Lloyd Praeger as a companion, it is impossible to look at a seal without Thomson's work appearing too. Much as he recounts meeting a travelling man, Peadar MacNamara, in Kerry who has news from Galway and Mayo and even of Thomson himself in Kerry the year before, his work is like hearing a succession of clear, unmuffled voices from around the island's coast. Voices that speak from a lifetime's close observation of the sea and the seals. Voices that speak from an existence embedded in the immediate environment. Voices that recount the depth of a life lived within a small, localised range. Voices that watched the world outside the window, watched what went on there, and acted accordingly. 'They will have knowledge of a storm before it breaks and then they'll lie close to the shore, or lie in to a creek.'[13]

Thomson tells one story, where a number of fishermen

are led out of a storm and saved by a seal, in which it is clear that the seal was viewed with respect and even a form of reverence. It is clear that there was no rupture between those on this island's coast and their natural environment. Of course, the seal, in both appearance and sound, has human-like qualities that appear to create a particular affinity but there can be no doubt that those who lived on and by the sea, who day in and day out saw the seals moving through the water and were familiar with their habits, attributed to the seal and in that way to the natural world, to the simple environment outside the back door, a credibility that infiltrated each aspect of their lives. 'We were always on good terms with the seals and close to them, and even in the old times, when you might win as much by killing a seal as now you would killing a pig, no man of the ferry would molest them . . . Those men that did had no luck after . . . I have heard my grandfather say "It is better to have nothing to do with seals unless you are willing to do well by them".'[14]

On this occasion I saw no seal. I watched the waves in the hope that the strangely familiar head might appear, the far-out swimmer, the native fisherman, but there was nothing. Again though, I was not disappointed, for I did not believe I could call them up, or that they would appear on demand. I left safely believing that one unsuspecting day I would see them again. 'Walk on their lonely beaches, climb on to their rocks with the knowledge that the sea before you stretches unbroken to America, that for thousands of years people believed what you now feel, that you are at the uttermost edge of the Earth, and when all is quiet except for waves and sea-birds you hear an old man gasp. You turn towards the sound. It is a seal.'[15]

And in the sun's ray through the glass
lifting towards the low noon, I
am bound.[1]

Roy Fisher

10

A Murmuration

There is an old man who wheezes and whistles in the yard. And when I look up it is a starling. At the coast, where the swallows arrive and depart and the seal unpredictably shows its face, I did not expect to see, moving unevenly across the fields, a small flock of starlings. Rumbustious, rolling low across the grass and flying off with squawks of discordant noise, even knowing these birds can turn up here from as far away as Russia, I still think of them as birds from the city. Seeing them on the headland leaves me with a feeling of dislocation. It is as if the starlings have brought the city with them.

In the yard, every summer, starlings nest and next door, in the rundown space of another farmyard, they nest too, amongst peeling walls of corrugated iron. In the yard itself they nest in the eaves of a bedraggled outhouse. The parent birds fly in and out as the summer progresses and inside the eaves the sound of young nestlings gets progressively louder. I have waited and watched, sat and looked, but I have never managed to see the young leave the nest. I have never seen the fluffed greyness, the mismatch of downy colours that gave rise at one time to a belief that the young bird was a different species. Somehow these yard birds seem completely wild. They share nothing here but the space between the eaves. They are not as present as the robin, for instance, or the blackbird. They do not approach as close as an arm's width like the blue and great tits do at a winter peanut feeder. The starlings are distant, remote, taking advantage of the buildings but disappearing as soon as the young join them outside the house. They rarely, if ever, come to the bird table. They certainly do not inhabit the concrete space of the yard the way the swallows do for the length of a whole summer. The way the chittering, complaining, beautiful blackbird does. I still recognise them, however. I still know them, or if not them, these wilder, less approachable ones, their kind. For if the blackbird brings a touch of the sacred to the backyard, then the starling brings, well, the starling brings to the backyard a touch of the backyard.

If this book is about place, if it is truly about Patrick Kavanagh's assertion that one field is as much as one can fully experience, then I cannot discuss the field without discussing the city and I cannot discuss the city without discussing the starling. I do not mean to go to the city, not physically anyway – this book is still about that small radius outwards from the backdoor of the farmhouse – but when I see the starling I see the city. The city is in the yard, too.

I grew up in the city and the starling was a part of the streets. I grew up in the places those 1950s' emigrants, the ones that John Banville watched so long ago, the ones who made their way along that straight road, went to. Birmingham and London, Manchester and Glasgow. Perhaps when they saw the starlings they were reminded of the fields and the yards and the headlands, much as I am now reminded of the city. It goes around and around and there is always company.

It was winter when we watched the starlings. At the same time every day, around four o'clock or half past. When the city streets were truly beginning to darken, when the street lights were coming on, when the roads began to fill with tired people making their way home. The people would all be coming out of the city and passing along the city streets and the old roads of inner city houses and out into the rings of the suburbs. They would have been passing the streets where most of those emigrants, once they had left those meandering lanes and that straight road, had ended up. They would have been leaving them behind. The starlings, the quarrelsome, disputatious starlings, would be going the other way from the flow out of the city: they would all be going in.

Sometimes a smaller group might pass over first. Sometimes right over the house, sometimes to the left, sometimes to the right. Sometimes it might just be the noise of them as they passed further down or further up the street. Sometimes a large flock would pass over and it would appear that that was all there would be. Always though, the vast gathering would come. Each and every afternoon, each and every winter's evening, the starlings would pass overhead on their way to a numberless roost in the city centre. The sky would fleck black and the noise easily cover the constant, unsettled rumble of the city. Over and over the house. On and on. I can trace them now, sitting here so far away, over the other side of the Irish Sea. They would be coming in from the east, from fields that border the city's edge, from sewage plants perhaps, from some abandoned, forgotten corners of rural land that linger by the expanding urban sprawl. They would be passing over high-rise flats and the city's edge, tough streets with pubs only a certain few go into, streets where those who didn't wish to reside where those 1950s' emigrants were, took flight to. They would pass over them. They would pass through the suburbs where tidiness and gentility rested. Where the treetop blackbird hid beside a garage door. They would pass over roads where cars lined up and lights moved and people came and went and came and went. Up in the sky the starlings would be dancing their way through the city streets, over and past a geography that would be to them just like any other geography, with a choreography like any other choreography, beneath their own inimitable choreography. The concrete field just like the headland one. Nature flowing over the built and the unbuilt. Above the city, a murmuration of starlings.

The collective term 'murmuration' for a flock of starlings could not be more apt for, apart from those vast congregations, one of the most striking features of the starling is its voice. Where the blackbird's voice is beautiful, almost at times preciously so, the starling's is nothing short of strange. Not that it does not possess beauty, too, and more than once I have been momentarily fooled, as the starling's endless mimicry begins with a few bars of a blackbird's song, before collapsing into the gurgles and wheezes that are its true voice. 'A lively rambling medley of throaty warbling, chirruping, clicking, and gurgling sounds interspersed with musical whistles and pervaded by a peculiar creaky quality.'[2] In the yard a beautifully spotted, sheeny starling can be seen from time to time perched halfway up a tree, always a tree overhanging the concrete yard for some reason, clicking and wheezing. It has none of the yellow-beaked fragility of the beautiful blackbird. None of that uplifting air. It does sound like humour, though, like a laugh. The starling sounds not unlike joy.

At the huge roost in the city the noise is there, too. If I

stand in the yard a moment and watch the starling singing I am taken back and I am in a different geography, one far away from here, one urban and heavy. One still rooted, however, still fixed, cemented by the starling's song. I also notice, cannot help noticing, that the bird is always around the rundown yard, that it is there I always see it. Can the city dweller not leave the concrete alone even when it pitches up here in the country? Or is it that I only note it when I can put it in that context? The starling, the humble, often maligned starling, is creating an intellectual and emotional hinterland that in many ways overrides geography. In this case the starling but, in general, nature itself, sets up an equivalent ecosystem in the human mind, an ecosystem where the human becomes part of a bigger, truer, more complete picture.

In the city those vast roosts topple over ledges and on to a few urban treetops. Thousands and thousands of birds line the city streets. Before settling in they have swooped and soared, they have coalesced in black clouds, split apart in thunderous showers. They have danced and swayed above the city streets, the buses and the cars, the homeward-bound workers and the flickering lights. They have moved to beats and signals we cannot hear or see. Ironically, this is all before starling roosts became a televisual wildlife spectacle, became commodified as entertainment. 'The way they formed huge shoals and then broke away and merged once more always took the breath away. After many fly-pasts and fragmentations they would land. Behind the neon signs . . .'[3] Sadly though, those huge city roosts, those thousands of birds I watched flying over our inner city house at the same time day after day, are truly a thing of the past. Netting over building ledges and chemical repellents sought to chase the birds away. Those vast spectacles were deemed a nuisance, were judged to be unhygienic and injurious to public health. 'Are we really too tidy to live with one of nature's wonders?'[4] Above our heads the unmistakable wonder of a vast starling roost was a civic detriment. On television it is a public attraction.

Even cleansed and tidied the yard is a shabby affair. On one side a low, fairly wide outhouse. Then, on the other side of the concrete yard, grass stubbornly sticking up through the joining lines of the slabs, an old stable. Adjoining it, a two-storey outbuilding with the slates falling away. It is faded now, weather and time worn, even with being maintained year after year. It does not look as if it ever emitted any sense of grandeur. These are working buildings. They are utilities. They were not constructed to impress. This unassuming concrete yard is still important though. 'Vernacular buildings are often the only source of information on life and landscapes of households of more modest or poorer circumstances . . . They are ordinary, everyday, workaday constructions by craftsmen, tapping into their local culture and heritage, and intimately connected with the environmental resources of their locality.'[5] There is a silent testimony here amongst this crumbling whitewash and these corrugated roofs.

The buildings were probably constructed sometime in the last century when the farm was able to expand a little. They would have been built, as the 1845 map of the cluster of twelve structures shows, where other buildings had once stood. Perhaps the remains were knocked down to make room. Perhaps the old building materials were reused. Perhaps one layer went on top of another. Immediately I am back again amongst the forgotten stories and the vanished lives. I wonder what lies beneath the buildings. Not in terms of foundation and structure but what really lies beneath them. 'The stories of the vernacular places of poorer classes (which make up most of the landscape) are mainly to be excavated out of the material landscape itself.'[6] Which make up most of the landscape. It rings in my ears. If I do not look at the rundown outhouse I am only grasping a portion of the landscape's story. The smallest portion. Who lived in the twelve buildings and where did they go? I do not mean what were their names and their occupations. I do not mean to go on a genealogical search. I mean who were they? Are they part of the long line whose presence is felt now by their absence? The serfs of the Gaelic order, the Famine victims, the landless labourers, the 1950s' Irish sailing away. 'House ruins in derelict and abandoned uplands and marginal lands of the west highlight where fields and farms, lanes and boreens have long surrendered to fern and briar in the face of emigration.'[7] Did these original buildings fall away when the lane below was altered, when the gorse was planted? What chased these people away? Famine and fear, perhaps. Or the lure of a better life overseas. Or progress. Improvement measures that did not include them. On a cool evening like this, the new year stumbling forward, the worst of the winter hopefully spent, did they gather around the fires of this place? Did they come out into this yard? Did their children play here? Did they look out from doorways into this same space? I do not know. I do not have any way of knowing. They are gone and all I have are the failing buildings that replaced them. I have their absence. 'The tens of thousands of landless labourers in pre-famine Ireland typically occupied one-roomed cabins made of mud or sod, which were classically bio-degradable and have literally melted from the Irish landscape, in many cases with the class that built them.'[8]

On those wet days, usually in winter but often throughout the year, this yard runs with water and soil washed away from the fields up above. The water washes away along the full length of the lane and down on to the road where it disappears into a gully. Sometimes it overflows and the passage of the water lies for days afterwards leaving a clear trace of where it came from.

The starlings nest early in the yard. Even before the swallows have returned they are disappearing in and out of the gap above one of the windows on the long outbuilding. The nest is messy and bits of straw stick out and fall to the ground. This most gregarious of birds becomes for the nesting period a solitary pair. As the summer begins and the young can be heard inside, the starlings are busier and busier. They fly to and from the yard. Then one morning the young have ventured out and the starlings are gone. They do not stay around like the swallow. They no longer fly around the outhouses. There are no young starlings to be seen on beams or overhanging wires inside the buildings for the rest of the summer. They nest and then they go. My city birds do not linger long in the farmyard.

Outside the city I have never seen those huge roosts although I know they take place in the country too and now, hunted from the city, they probably only take place there. Yet it is not just that the starling is gone from those city roosts, no longer flies over those city streets and over that house from which I watched it, it is now the case that the starling too is said to be in decline. The guidebooks here still describe it as common and present in all counties and it is truly not difficult to see a starling. Like others, though – the kestrel, the herring gull, the swallow, common birds, common to our everyday lives – the decline is alarming. Why would a bird described in a 1976 guide as 'superabundant'[9] be in a 2005 guide described as suffering from 'huge declines', with numbers falling by '60 per cent over the last

25 years'.[10] I look out at the now cold concrete of the yard and think of this, think again of Rachel Carson's warnings and wonder again how much were they were listened to? Truly listened to? How could the common starling decline in such a way? And what of the others? What, in fact, of the bird most closely associated with the starling in the urban mind? What of the house sparrow, a bird that seems to have followed humanity across the globe, seems to have spread as we have spread, is as tied to us through history as any other aspect of our environment, which is now facing a decline in numbers of up to 60 per cent? What are we to think? That this is only happening over there, over in those big conurbations to which those 1950s' emigrants went? Are we to think that, like them, it is removed from our lanes and fields? I watch the house sparrows each year at the front of the house. Even after the front of the house had had to have repairs to stop the fascia board completely disintegrating, the sparrows merely created another hole where the old one had been and nested again. They flew in and out of the hole, only yards away from us in the sunshine, oblivious and unperturbed by our presence. In time the noise of the young inside, a noise that often marked the beginning of a day, was combined with their heads peeking out of the nest site, out of the house in which they were born. Forget the enduring raven and the returning swallow: if any bird is faithful to us it is the sparrow. Faithful to us since humans first began to spread out across the globe. Faithful to us since we first began to settle. Faithful to us to the extent that some of the ones born in the outside walls of this house may well live their entire lives, lives that can last as long as ten years, just yards from this house. Faithful so that apart from brief forays into the surrounding fields, this house and this yard will constitute the entirety of their existence. Perhaps here in

Ireland the house sparrow remains as common as it always was but even if the decline is only happening overseas it is enough. Even if the decline is not happening here in the nest site freshly made in the wall of the house. Even if it is not here in this yard. Even if those cities over the water are far away from these fields. For the imaginative hinterland the starlings and sparrows create, the association with city streets and city roosts that they bring here to this yard in the countryside of Ireland, is mirrored by a biological one. Across the Irish Sea is our ecological neighbour. Nature is not aware of our political borders. Biology does not adhere to the imposed constructs of our accepted international reality. So the disappearing sparrows across the short width of the Irish Sea are doing so in a bioregion that is not too remote from that of our own sparrows. Nature's territories follow their own outlines. 'Is the house sparrow today's equivalent of the miner's canary? Is something nasty going on in our towns that might affect us all?'[11]

There is, as they say here, a fine stretch in the evenings now. Almost without noticing it the year has turned. Suddenly the evenings are light. The weather is as it always is and the Atlantic is never far from offering a reminder that it is close by. Still, the lanes will be brighter now, warmer. The days will offer more again. The fields and the sea cliffs will open up again.

I am not being disingenuous, however, when I say that the setting, the rolling contours of this corner of the Irish countryside, are only important because this is where I happen to be living. When I stood in the yard and thought of the city I realised that this book could have been written there too. Gary Snyder's city streets could carry the wilderness, and so could mine. Perhaps that is why I like the concrete, messy yard so much, because it reminds me of the city; nature breaking through the sterility, blossoming. The toughness of the starling, the insistence of the sparrow. This is my locality now. This is where my backdoor is. But the city was that place once. My backdoor was there once. A locality can be anywhere. 'The weeds in a city lot convey the same lesson as the redwoods.'[12] That city book would be different, would take different paths and have a different emphasis. It would have no seals and, I suspect, no otters. It would have others, though. It could be traced. It would be just as truthful. There would be kestrels on the school roof. Hedgehogs on a concrete path. Foxes. There would be city pigeons instead of rock doves. There would be house sparrows, I hope. And there would be those huge starling fly-overs and swirling roosts above city buildings, even if only in memory. I would be with those 1950s' emigrants again and that would be a book too.

There is a great poet of the city and it so happens that he is a poet of the very city across the Irish Sea where I first saw those starlings and watched a house sparrow on a fence and never caught sight of a swallow. I walk away from the yard and there is a circle again and company. 'The universe, we define/as that which is capable of having/a place like this for its centre./There's no shame/in letting the world pivot/on your own patch.'[13]

Philosophy is a place-based exercise. It comes from the body and the heart and is checked against shared experience.[1]

Gary Snyder

11

The Shape and the Testimony

When it is nest-building time, the house tells me. I lie awake in the mornings and hear it. I listen to the walls. In the double chimney, above and beside the bedroom, the jackdaws are building their nest.

The 1845 map of these lands shows a cluster of twelve buildings. Some of these may have been outhouses but it is more likely that these were dwelling places, a cluster of homes and people. It might have been a place where such dwellings had been for upwards of 200 years, though there is in essence no real way of knowing this. The memory of it has gone. There are no substantial records. The history of the land, even at this localised level, remains the history of a certain section, of particular people, of an elite. History itself is the elite narrative. The lives of those twelve buildings were lived here however, within this space, contained by the footfalls that radiate away from the yard. Patrick Duffy talks of how the shape of the landscape was 'preserved in local memory and bolstered by periodic traversing by local tenants'.[2] In this way the very footsteps of those who lived here created the boundaries and the lanes. They created the shape and perimeter of the townland. They made the shape of this land. They made their own world. That is the vocabulary of landscape that lies outside this house. Those lives are gone and the details of their existence gone too. The basic mud-and-sod homes they lived in are gone. Nothing of their material existence remains. Something remains, though. The shape of their existence is here.

Not too far from here, out of the door and across the concrete yard, down the gorse-lined lane and along the straightness of the road, lie the remains of a handball alley. A game. A sport. Some three years ago, on the night of a storm that blew the roof off outbuildings and uprooted trees, the walls of the alley were blown over. The handball alley was gone. Much further away, on the road through the village that leads to the headland, another handball alley stood. It lay at the back of a derelict school. The school has been bought now and the building refurbished. That alley is gone now too. Peter Somerville-Large writes of those alleys that the 'handball courts served the really poor who could not afford hurley sticks'.[3] I know nothing of handball and know of no one who knows it. Knows of it, yes, but not anyone that knows it, the way these lanes and fields know football and hurling. A simple game, once played just over the fields from here, is now part of the forgotten detail. It is another part of the lost narrative. I do not know who went there to play. I do not know those who took themselves down to the handball court and what social stratification was implied by their playing that game. Were those courts really the preserve of the poor? The poor of a poor society? The handball courts would have been a part of society long after those twelve buildings stood here and they are separated by many, many years. They would have marked different landscapes. They do share things, however, apart from their geographical identity. I do not know who lived at the top of the lane in those twelve buildings and what they thought or spoke of on an evening or a morning standing in the yard where I so often stand. I do not know, as I have said, who went down to the handball alley to play. I do not know. I have to be simply content with knowing that they existed. I have to be content with the outline. I have to be content with knowing less than I would wish. I have to be content with knowing less than they deserve. But I have the shape. The landscape itself is that. Their existence is here. The landscape is their testimony.

This house, too, offers a link. It is still here, still creating this space as a dwelling space, offering a shape. It is likely that pre-Famine days saw the house begin to take shape. Someone would have lived here then. The house would have been one storey, or perhaps a divided two, of low rooms. Later, other pieces were added on; another floor, more rooms, a still-standing byre, leaning against the back. There would not have been then, outside a narrow elite, any great material inequalities in terms of housing but the house would have marked something. Some humble flag of standing. Certainly by the time it became a single farm it had. Certainly by the time it took the shape it had now. It would have marked a new social standing across the landscape. It would have marked, too, the demise of the old one, the one the map shows it was so closely linked to. It is all here. In the fields and in the stones. The shape and the testimony.

They drop a lot of sticks, the jackdaws, and they make a lot of noise. They are both in and above the chimney. Twice over the last four or five summers I have had to remove from the sooty base of the fireplace a young bird, his black more deeply blackened by the fall down the chimney. The birds themselves, however, have been unharmed, small but as bright of beady eye as their parents, eyes blue instead of pearl grey, and I have been able to return them to a height where they can be safe. I thought the ravens showed such great fidelity but of a kind that was deliberately distanced from us. I thought the swallows showed a fidelity that was directly linked to us, was a return from so far away to the same ledges on the same joists, year after year. I thought of the sparrows, of their insistent proximity. The starling from the city and the blackbird from the forest. But what of the jackdaws? What of these birds that, year after year, disturb my morning sleep because we live inside the same house? The jackdaws and I inhabit the same place. If I do not know them can I really know my own home?

Roderic O'Flaherty, who stood and watched the gannets diving as I did more than 300 years later, was a member of a native society that was in the process of losing its status and power. Nevertheless, O'Flaherty's writings suggest that he never stopped seeking to know his own country, to have knowledge of his surroundings. 'O'Flaherty's knowledge of geography and natural history is particularly extensive. He knows the source of each river, the families of each townland, their genealogy, patrimony, extent and history of their property, its acquisition and loss. He describes the mountains, lakes, soil and its agricultural productions.'[4] These are the only things I know about Roderic O'Flaherty but in that sense I know a lot, for in this instance O'Flaherty's knowledge, his learning, his interests allow me to see him. His immersion in his surroundings reveals him. O'Flaherty's landscape is his biography.

The English poet John Clare was so completely a poet of his own place, so attuned to it, so at home there, that moving only three miles away could be said to have finally broken his mind. Clare's locality is undoubtedly his biography. Encouraged by well-meaning friends to move out of the village where he had been born and had lived his whole life, to a better cottage, Clare suffered. 'I've left mine old home of homes/Green fields and every pleasant place/The summer like a stranger comes.'[5] He was eventually to spend over twenty-two years in an asylum. During one period of hospitalisation he escaped and walked all the way to his home place, navigating by the sun. Clare had not only been unable to cope with literary acclaim and the leaving of home but he had lived through the enclosures, when the common lands of his native Britain disappeared. He had felt this deep alteration keenly. 'Fence now meets fence on owners' little bounds/Of field and meadow large as garden grounds/In little parcels little minds to please.'[6]

Like Roderic O'Flaherty, knowing the source of rivers and all the families of a townland, John Clare, some hundred-odd years later and on the other side of the Irish Sea, knew best his own place. Another hundred-odd years later and Jack Sheehan, not too far along the coast from here, lived a life, too, that could be encompassed by an afternoon's walk. It is not that these three of many, three who have left some kind of record behind, lived small, cramped lives but that they lived in true proximity to their immediate surroundings. To their lanes and hills, to the rivers and the grasses, to the birds that flew over and the animals that passed by. In this way they knew fully where they lived. It was said of John Clare that he was a 'miniaturist, the inhabiter of locality',[7] that his entire inspiration was 'the expiration of his beloved places'.[8] He lived and breathed his own patch of place. The three miles he moved seem trifling distances by most standards but so entwined was Clare with his surroundings that the distance was enough to cut him adrift.

He left his home and was lost. Now John Clare may be a somewhat singular example and may be too easy to interpret as an intense poet of locality whose loss of sanity coincided with environmental and personal changes. It runs the risk of sounding too glib. Looking at his work, though, and the known history of his life, it would seem strange not to make these assumptions. For Clare the 'interior order of the human mind was inextricable from the environmental space which we inhabit'[9] and this led to the undoing of his mental state. It does not lessen the potency of that relationship. The fact that it was his undoing does not mean it was any less the essence of his person. Roderic O'Flaherty, John Clare and Jack Sheehan, all different, all from different localities and all experiencing different geographies, represent the same instances and the same impulse. They went outside the backdoor and looked around and found that it was enough.

In Ireland many assumptions are made about the relationship we have with nature. The Irish, it is said, are a post-colonial people and when they look at the fields and hills they do so from colonised minds, minds infected with a deep self-disregard. So the land is loved, the ownership of it is loved, but it is not valued. It is disregarded. See the quiet glory of a country lane and see, too, the country lane littered with rubbish; a carpet, a television. There is no reason, of course, to believe that earlier Irish societies were in any way removed from their natural environment. They had as intimate a relationship with nature as earlier societies anywhere. But the forests went and the wolves and the goshawks. A Gaelic society collapsed. The people were estranged from their land. Then came the Great Famine. For the Irish people, for Irish society, 'in the biological treachery of the famine', Michael Viney writes, 'nature was disgraced'.[10] Nature was disgraced. Irish society was now, at best, ambivalent to nature. At worst, it was hostile. These are our assumptions when we look at the land. There was a division. 'Before and after the Famine, the inhabitants of the Big House and its demesne exercised a surplus biblical dominion over nature stretching beyond utility and necessity into aesthetics, leisure and connoisseurship . . . the native population had more pragmatic anxieties.'[11] So when interest in science exploded, when nature became something to be studied, to be categorised, to be written about, those writing in post-Famine, end-of-colonial Ireland were all members of a certain section of society. Robert Lloyd Praeger, Ellen Hutchins, J. P. Burkitt, Richard Ussher. For others the natural world was not something to be aesthetically enjoyed. It was not something worthy of close exploration. Even the place-rooted, rural sensibilities of Patrick Kavanagh revealed this. 'O stony grey soil of Monaghan,/The laugh from my love you thieved.'[12] These are our assumptions. Yet at the same time Jack Sheehan was imbibing the depth of his Sheep's Head farm. The collectors of the Folklore Commission were recording a wealth of local, rooted, connections.

Throughout earlier years of turmoil Roderic O'Flaherty wrote intensely about the natural environment, field labourers sang a Gaelic lament for the fallen forests, Amhlaoibh Ó Súilleabháin wrote closely detailed natural history observations in his native Irish language and when David Thomson arrived years later on the Atlantic seaboard he found a vibrant sea life culture. Patrick Kavanagh, too, may have deplored the stony grey soil but he also wrote of his land in another way. Kavanagh, much like Clare, had a love of the land that existed beyond reflection. 'The burnet saxifrage was there in profusion/And the autumn gentian/I knew them all by eyesight long before I knew their names./We were in love before we were introduced.'[13] They are all there. There is more to this country's relationship with nature than our assumptions. Whilst attempting this open air literature I have found company everywhere. Every walk has been done in company. The landscape is not just a text in itself but is often an already translated one.

Simon Schama writes that 'landscape is the work of the mind'.[14] The company I have found walking these hills and cycling these lanes is testimony to the truth of that. I am always seeing through the eyes of others. It is also, quite literally, true that the land is the work of the mind for materially, physically, the Ireland we have before us is shaped by mankind. Very, very little of this country has not been affected by the activities of generation after generation of people. The land has been shaped by us. It has been felled by us. It has been enclosed by us. It has been farmed by us. It has been planted by us. It is now even being formed by us. The contour of the land dictated by us. A hill removed there. A hill created there. An estate here. A motorway there. The landscape is indeed the work of our minds. Simon Schama also writes that 'landscapes are culture before they are nature; constructs of the imagination projected onto wood and water and rock'.[15] On this occasion, however, he is wrong. The land is always nature before it is anything else. Physically that is true and culturally that is true, too. The land has been translated many times but somewhere lies the original text and a glimpse of that is still part of our experience of nature. Sometimes we have to see around and beyond those who have gone before. Sometimes it is desirable for the artists and poets, the writers and the scientists, to move aside. To get out of the way. Let the view be the view. Indeed, there is a time when the writers and poets should be willing to say nothing. Should, in fact, recognise silence as the most appropriate response. Nature should be, as far as possible, directly experienced, not filtered through words or images or ideas. Those words and images and ideas, so many of them enriching and beyond value, should come later. We only need the company if we have first set out alone. We need to begin by opening the backdoor. We should recognise that nature is not a construct of our imagination. It is not something we have projected on to the land. When we accept that, we can let the peregrine falcon stoop for itself, we can let the otter swim and the blackbird sing. We can let the joy of the swallow flying over the yard be simply that. We can still acknowledge that 'the old Gaelic vernacular has been lost to most of the country, and with it a range of names for plants and animals, the key to the old Gaelic community's relationship with the natural world. The decline of that primitive relationship with land and sea, and the extinction of its vocabulary'[16] and accept that as part of our experience of nature on this island. We can accept Douglas Hyde's assertion that 'the unique stock-in-trade of an Irish-speaker's mind' is 'gone forever, and replaced by nothing'.[17] We can accept all of that. The response, however, lies not just in the unearthing of those lost minds and those lost words but in the land itself, to what Seán Lysaght termed the 'innocent landscape'.[18] What has been lost has been lost but what can be experienced is still there, still just over the hill, around the bend. Still just outside the backdoor. When the blackbird sings it demands only to be listened to. When the peregrine swoops it deserves only to be watched. When the swallow flies it needs us only to look up. Then, as Seamus Heaney says, we can go 'back home, still with nothing to say/Except that now you will uncode all landscapes/By this: things founded clean on their own shapes,/Water and ground in their extremity.'[19]

Things founded clean on their own shapes. If we were instead to reside with Simon Schama's view of nature as a manuscript that we can not only explain but that, by and large, we compiled, then we remain at a remove. We do not open the backdoor. We do not go down the lanes. We do not lean in and smell the rich, sweet coconut of the tough gorse. We are not part of the land, we are the housed spectators. Not only that but we are forever stuck in a Baconian position of superiority, where nature is merely a utility we can exploit. Not only do we create it, fully decipher and understand it, we do with it what we will. One position breeds the other. Indeed, are they not the very ways of thinking that have led us to the ecological position we are now in? Is that not the mindset that has led us here, to the environmental condition we find the world in? Simon Schama's intimation that the land only exists when we look at it leaves us outside of the organic whole. It leads on to a whole way of being in the land. It rejects an entire other way of looking at and understanding the sights outside the kitchen window, a few steps from the backdoor. I do not wish to feel that way when I step down the lane. I do not want to see in that way. I prefer to think of myself as a part of what I see. I prefer to be part of the organic whole. I prefer the 'idea that we can make no firm ontological divide in the field of existence: that there is no bifurcation in reality between the human and the non-human realms . . . to the extent that we perceive boundaries, we fall short of deep ecological consciousness'.[20]

Every text that I have delved into in order to explore this patch of earth has been of wonderful value. Each one has been a pleasure to discover. I have welcomed each mind I have met. Yet I stand in the lanes and the fields, look out from the headland or watch from the yard and I recognise Aldo Leopold's call for 'intellectual humility' when dealing with nature and recognise, too, the truth of his words that nature and wilderness give 'definition and meaning to the human enterprise'.[21] So, even accepting Foster's assertion that in terms of nature the 'Irish experience has been marked by . . . discontinuity, exile and sterility'[22] and even acknowledging that it is more than difficult not to mediate nature, difficult not to look out from a place of discontinuity and exile, difficult not to see from the experience of others, to see what has already been seen, to be aware that others will see through what we experience, even accepting all this, I still believe that none of it should get in the way. I believe the essential worth lies in what is before my eyes. 'Locked in the prison-house of language, dwelling in the *logos* not the *oikos*, we know only the text, not the land. Unless, that is, we could come to understand that every piece of land is itself a text, with its own syntax and signifying potential. Or one should say: come to understand once again, as our ancestors did. For the idea that the earth itself is a text is a very old one.'[23]

There is no harm in being aware of all those other minds, in hearing all those other voices. Indeed, having that knowledge can only enrich us. But nature can still mean simply looking out or looking up. As Richard Mabey writes, it is all part of it. 'Landscape, as a language is pure pidgin. It's full of slang, neologisms, mimicry and faddish jargon, yet with the odd knack of being comprehensible.'[24] 'Simply looking', though, they must always remain the first words.

The jackdaws build the nest simply by dropping sticks into the nest space until enough of them catch and begin to build up. Their habit of doing this in chimneys means it is not hard to know they are around. And, of course, there is the call, the repetitive, early morning yap echoing around the yard. These jackdaws live with us as much as it is possible to do so. This is their home too. When the swallows are far away, the starlings have departed their temporary lodgings and even the sparrows are more on the bird table than the house, the jackdaws still appear around the chimney. They still appear in a tree looking on and the more I find out about them the more I feel connected to them.

Here, in the beauty of the countryside, I find that my surroundings are again biography for, like the fleeting starlings and like me, the jackdaw knows another landscape. 'It flourishes particularly in the modern landscape, taking advantage of a whole spectrum of industrial and urban settings, such as rubbish tips, factory dumps, motorway service stations and the motorway verge itself.'[25] The jackdaw knows an underbelly of society that seems very far away from here. The jackdaw in the farmhouse chimney is a reminder that the city streets and the rubbish dumps, the factory and the motorway, are places too and that nature is as much there as elsewhere. Those places are the earth too. Here I watch the jackdaws standing on a ridge of grass in a farmyard amongst rolling hills and fields. Others have seen them elsewhere. 'I have seen these sociable, cheerful birds strutting jauntily in village streets in Anglesey, perching and chattering on the stone walls outside the grounds of Blarney Castle, and fluttering around the square at Tulcea on the Danube delta.'[26] Like me, the jackdaw is as at home here as it is amongst the bleak byways of a modern landscape. This house, this yard, these hills are simply home on this occasion.

Around the place they are wary without being distant. They perch openly on fence posts when some task or other is being undertaken, curious, wondering if a food source is about to turn up. Watching a jackdaw is to be watched back. That grey eye looking out at as blatantly as I look back. What looks at me is nature. What sounds in the chimney in spring or out in the yard on a grey afternoon is nature. I have not constructed the jackdaw. I have not created it. It did not wait for my eye to come into being. If I look out at this admittedly human-altered land and do not see such trifles as that beady eye looking back, then perhaps the landscape is only a construct of my imagination, is first and foremost culture. It is what humanity has made it. Only if I choose not to see, however. Only if I choose not to hear. Only if I do not awake in the morning to the jackdaws a few feet above me. Only if I do not see them moving in the sky around me. Only if I decide to know a certain amount rather than all I can. Indeed, such is the jackdaws' belonging here that they know contours of air and shapes of wind above and around the house, that are beyond me. In that way they 'play in the wind, fully aware of distance and the local air conditions. They allow the wind to throw them upwards, then, with a casual flap of the wings, turn over, momentarily opening their pinions and then dive. The wind protects the jackdaw through the air at over eighty miles an hour with the birds never out of control'.[27] They know the local air. If I don't see them, what do I see?

When the winter comes the jackdaws join with rooks in a huge flock that passes over the house each evening. A few fields away a stand of conifers that marks some kind of landscape feature on a golf course is the night-time roost of thousands of birds. A mixed flock of crows make their bed there each night. One cold evening, I go out into the field that slopes above the house and climb up. I promised myself during the winter that one evening I would be out when the flock passes over. I walk through the crackling stubble and towards the solid yet bare mark of the ditch. Some kind of shelter, I think, will be best so that the birds do not see me and do not fly so as to avoid me. I stand beside the winter bareness of a ditch and although the thorns are bare now and the outline of the hedgerows is traced in the air they are solid enough to hide me. It is cold. Looking down along the line of the lane I can see across the uneven shapes of the fields, fields formed long ago by forgotten divisions of family and spade, fields created by births and by deaths. I know that in the distance where the fields begin to sweep up again and the land rises steadily lies the black line of the river and somewhere there, too, the vanished line of a railway that once lead through these townlands and down to the coast. Little of that railway now remains, certainly little away from the main line. Still, the curious corners of local history can be found and I smile knowing of the hidden house over there that lies next to the river, below the ruined castle and in the middle of a field and lane network, and I smile because it is called Railway Cottage. On a line of trees by the old schoolhouse I can see that jackdaws have gathered. I think at first it is purely a gathering of the smaller crows but higher up a tree, a tree further in from the road, are the rooks. The birds are dotted throughout the trees, on branches higher and lower and while there is a constant noise and constant movement there is nothing of chaos about them. Far off to the left, from the direction of the main road, I can see some flocks moving in the air, sweeping across the evening sky. I watch them, watch the groups coming in ones and twos, watch the smaller groups that break away and fly over the fields towards the roost. At the same time I am watching my nearby jackdaw gathering so that I do not miss the moment of departure. When it comes, of course, it comes at no discernible signal. Considering these birds can judge the air enough to ride the movements of it, it is hardly surprising that their group communication is invisible to me. Suddenly there are streams and streams, broad bands of black birds passing over. They are not high. Most evenings they pass over the house at just above roof height. For a moment I am underneath them and in the darkness of the hedge I hear them calling, hear the movement of their wings, feel them in the air. I hear flight. Above me and in the wintering sky they fly across the star-shining horizon. They fly, tonight, slowly and gracefully. On other nights, as they pass me standing by the backdoor, they swirl and move in the wind with ease and exuberance. They are heavy and dark but they fly with a solid grace. In Mark Cocker's wonderful evocation of nature and place he describes this gathering as having 'the beauty of common purpose'[28] and even the odd straggler, the black shape following on through solitary space, still seems part of the group. In the same work he talks, too, of rookeries that go back as much as 300 years, the use and suitability of them handed down through generations of birds. Watching these birds now I am struck again by nature's fidelity. Each winter's evening I have been in this farmhouse these birds have passed over and for how many years before that?

'Few native animals in North America have been so fiercely persecuted as the Common Crow'[29] and this family of birds has 'suffered a form of compound odium and persecution'.[30] These are two of the things that come to mind as I watch their night-time flight. I think, too, of the strong possibility that totemic species such as eagles and kites have fallen prey here to poisoned bait left out for 'vermin' such as crows. If these are unloved, I think, if for centuries these assorted crows have been despised as vermin, poisoned and shot, what is it that we did not see? Is this roost really not a thing to marvel at? On a winter's evening as I move around the house or open the backdoor to see if the rain has stopped the noise of the roost is carried down the fields. I hear the social structure of the crows asserting itself. In the winter the house jackdaws are almost certainly over there. In the winter

I hear them going to bed. In the spring I hear them getting up.

It is said of pairs of jackdaws, like the pair that wake me in the morning, that they 'defend each other loyally and are seldom separated, remaining together during their lifetimes and not even separating during the winter when they join wandering flocks'.[31] How long has this particular couple been nesting here? Or are these descendants? And where are the ones I took out of the fireplace – are they here too? Is this a family of birds that will go back generations like John Clare's Raven's nest or Damien Enright's millennium-strong genetic chain? At the very least, these unloved birds are a continuity and a fidelity, a truth I cannot ignore.

Somebody and some part of the house is awake. The day begins.

*The hardest thing of all to
see is what is really there.*[1]

J. A. Baker

12

As if the Bow Had Flown
Off with the Arrow

The natural world is random. These days I am
beginning to scan the skies again. I know it is early
yet but my gaze goes upwards just in case a stray
swallow has arrived weeks and weeks earlier than usual. They
are sometimes recorded as doing so but I do not really expect
to see one. For some reason I am reminded of walking this
road one late summer's morning the year before, of glancing
casually up at the swallows flying around the field and seeing,
slightly higher and utterly distinctive in outline, a swift. As I
walk on I realise that there is a chapter about this bird
waiting. And the swift has flown into my pages. The natural
world is random.

One day in the city, many years ago, I was woken from
a deep sleep. The room was dark, heavily curtained, but I
knew from the rhythm and tenor of the air outside the
window that it was day. It took me a while to realise that it
was noises – specific, defined noises from inside the hall –
that had woken me. I lay a while and listened to them.

Something was trying to escape. I opened the door and whatever it was appeared to fall across the landing. I took a step up and the noise fell to the ground. At the top of the stairs, in a corner, a darkness crouched against the wall, crouched against the skirting board. Against the floor. A swift. Instantly, bizarrely, recognisable. It made no more attempts to fly as I stood there. I looked up and saw no open window, no obvious entry point. As to how or why it was there I do not know. I bent down and the swift making no attempt to move, no frightened fluttering, merely stilled a little more. I leant forward and took the bird in my hand. I placed my palm over its eyes and walked towards the door. I felt barely any weight in my hand, felt the angles of a skeletal outline, the slightest of scratchings from the short feet. At the door I halted and took a closer look. I had never seen and have not seen since a bird anything quite like the swift. The black appearance in the sky was revealed as being different hues of darkness. Black, brown, a pale patch on the chin. The scimitar wings. The eyes lying against the side of the head, wide and elongated, made for great heights and the curves of air, the spaces and boundaries of sky. This bird knew none of the flatness of vision that is my own. The face of the swift was like the face of a science fiction alien, the wings machine-like in their streamlined efficiency. It remained still, alert, very alive but unmoving, unresisting. Was it simply helpless, grounded in my palm? I opened the door and, my hand back over its eyes, I walked out. A few paces on I lifted away my hand and the swift lay in my palm and the sky lay above. For a moment nothing happened. I thought I might gently throw it, launch it back into the air. Perception then seemed to tremble in the bird. With the slightest of movements and the lightest of body tensing the swift left my open palm and me and went back to the sky. It moved and was gone. I watched its blackness ascend above the city street, fly once away from me until it had attained height and then swirl around and fly back over my head, the rooftop and into the sky. One of Gilbert White's 'shiftless beings'[2] had left me standing.

It is perhaps only fitting that the swift, so much a part of our natural environment and yet so alien, should belong to a bird family more remarkable and exotic than most of our other species. The swift is classified alongside the hummingbirds and therefore the resemblance it bears to our swallows and martins is regarded by biologists as being nothing more than convergent evolution. They have arrived at similar lives but in different ways, rather than from having close family ties. They have parallel lives but have come from different directions. Which, however true it is biologically, is true in other ways too, for if the swallow is always a neighbour, the swift is always a stranger. It is here like the swallow but not in the same way. Not in the same way at all. The swallow's life and its journeys, year after year, to and from this yard are the source of wonder for this book. They have been the point of beginning, the point of departure and the point of return. The hinterlands of its coming and going have been the geography of these pages. With the swift, though, it is the whole fact of its existence that is a thing of wonder. It is simply the swift itself that is the fascination. 'The most aerial of all birds: they invariably take their food in flight. They mate in flight (though also on the nest); drink and bathe flying low over the surface of the water; and except during the breeding season, spend the night on the wing,'[3] the guidebook tells me. I read through it again. They collect their nest-building material as it is blown about in the air. The young, after an unusually long incubation for a bird of this size, also stay in the nest for a long time, up to eight weeks. They mate in flight. Drink and bathe without landing. They spend the night on the wing. And there it is. That is the piece that tugs at me. They spend the night on the wing. They sleep in the air. I have read this before, not in a guide like this, in the literature of classification and description but in a work of fiction and as so often has happened in writing this open-air literature I am inside again searching through different books looking for the source. I am indoors looking along shelves. I am picking up book after book and I realise that I am searching for a short story I am not even sure exists. It is not where I thought it was and I am soon half-convinced I have imagined it. It is a story about a lost pilot during a war who comes across squadrons of swifts going around and around in the sky above the clouds. They are fast asleep. I cannot find it and I find no reference to it. I continue the hunt but begin to feel I have imagined it, that my mind has cobbled bits and pieces together, collected pieces blowing about in the air and created something unlikely. The most mysterious of birds to fly around and above these fields has led me here. The swift, of all birds the swift, the traceless one, the one that never comes down, has me hunkered in dusty corners, rooting into my own sense of belonging.

A writer who wrote entirely out of a deep sense of belonging and a yearning to fully know his own corner of land was the Englishman Gilbert White. White recorded in truly wonderful detail the natural history of his home village, with everything from spiders to deer, to frogs to old yew trees, catching his attention. Little escaped his eye, little seemed too insignificant to be examined. He walked and watched and recorded. He left nothing unobserved. Of his enduring fascinations, however, the birds that came to his village of Selborne every spring held a particular appeal. The swallows, the martins and the swifts. He was entranced by their summer intensity and their aerial life and of all these favourites it was the swift that most haunted him. 'The swift is White's true familiar,'[4] Richard Mabey noted.

Writing in the 1770s and 1780s Gilbert White undertook a careful investigation of the natural life of his neighbourhood, a neighbourhood he so intensely experienced that he died in the house he was born in, the house where he had lived nearly his entire life. He undertook his investigations with little more than his own eyes and a paper and pen. He studied what he termed 'common occurrences' and thought of his work as constituting a 'parochial history'.[5] He went out of his backdoor and discovered the world. In this parochial history, with its analysis of common occurrences, the swifts stood out. In these birds in particular, in their screaming freedom, White found a sense of longing. Although a rational and sceptical observer, White's searches amongst certain habitats for a proof that the swifts overwintered in some kind of state of hibernation reveals clear evidence of a desire that it be so. White wished for the swifts to stay. He wanted to think that they did not leave. It is not a desire that anyone who has watched swifts above a town street or screaming above a roof would find hard to understand. It is a desire I would easily recognise, remembering even in these cold, early days of spring, swifts above the church steeple in the town. The stray one on the late summer lane, the last swift of the year. Gilbert White found, of course, no evidence that the swifts remained. He settled instead for describing their departure, their early departure, long before the swallows and martins, as 'mysterious and wonderful' and especially recorded how quickly the helpless young are airborne and migrating and existing at the boundaries of our imagination. He looked at the young in the nest and wrote, 'we could not but wonder when we reflected that these shiftless beings in a little more than a fortnight would be able to dash through the air almost with the inconceivable swiftness of a meteor; and perhaps in their emigration must traverse vast continents and oceans as distant as the equator. So soon does nature advance small birds to their state of perfection.'[6] Gilbert White's imagination all those years ago was just about able to incorporate the idea of the swifts migrating vast distances. He was able to reach towards a true understanding of their nature simply by looking up at them. By leaning in closer to the nest. He was able, however reluctantly, to shake off older misinterpretations of their remarkable lives. He did not, in doing so, lose his abiding sense of wonder. The swifts, for him, remained mysterious and wonderful. They attained a state of perfection.

In many ways, of all the things encountered on leaving the backdoor, the swift is indeed the embodiment of wonder; the shiftless one in its state of perfection. If we did not wonder at the swift we would simply be lost. Even the bare details of its existence are a testimony to that. Swifts exist on what amounts to aerial plankton. Up to a few hundred metres above the ground there are masses of insects and web-borne spiders that exist in the air. This space is the pasturage of the swift. Stiff-winged, flying around in small screaming flocks, chasing one another over rooftops. As befits a creature of the air they are extremely sensitive to changes in the weather. Poor weather severely effects their food supply, reduces the numbers of those air-dwelling insects. If this bad weather comes during the summer, swifts will travel great distances to circumnavigate it, even in the middle of the breeding season. If a low-pressure weather front moves across the country, bringing rain with it, the swifts will simply fly around it and return at the back of it. This can involve very long distances, can bring the swift many, many miles away from the nesting site, but with most observers suggesting swifts can easily fly as much as 500 miles a day, that distance has a perspective. Ancestrally those nests would have been in clefts in caves and cliffs, perhaps in hollow dead trees, or the old holes of woodpeckers. Now they nest in cracks in the walls of tall buildings or in church steeples. Nesting, though, is an untypical part of their year, for this aside, the swift remains in the air. 'Except at the nest the swift's life is spent flying in a layer of air which stretches from just above the ground to fully 1,000ft above it.'[7] It is the bare simplicity of these facts that is most astonishing and like the screaming, thundering flight of a swift going past, too fast for the human eye to distinguish any pattern, the tumbling facts of its existence fall past me in a way that I am unable to order. Is it simply life in the unknown air above, harvesting unknown fields of insects, that is most astonishing? Is it the distances of daily flight, the ability to skip around bad weather? Or is it all the other details that fly past me? 'Swifts, for their size, are long lived, for individuals known to be nineteen and fifteen years old are on record; and these died not of old age, but from accidental causes.'[8] Nearly twenty years spent almost exclusively in the air. My mind stretches to fully comprehend that. Or that young swifts, soon after leaving the nest, are roosting on the wing, 'circling for hours in the cold night air at high altitude until morning. It is thought that immatures, which may not start to nest until their fourth year, may remain aloft for the whole of their early lives.'[9] They leave the nest and do not come down again from the sky for four years. Four years on the wing. Four years eating and drinking in the sky. Four years going around and around the sky at night asleep. Four years without the earth. Even in the nest, whilst the adult birds are perhaps circling around those weather patterns, the nestling swifts have a remarkable existence.

'Normally the parents take turns to incubate, but the eggs may be abandoned for several days without any harm coming to the embryo when the parents are forced to be absent. The young may also be left untended for long periods, relying entirely on their reserves of fat. If their fast is even further prolonged, the chicks temporarily lose control of their body temperature: that is, they become 'cold-blooded' and lapse into a sort of torpor which allows them to survive until nourishment is once more available. It appears that the adults also become torpid when food is scarce.'[10]

A sort of torpor. Birds existing in a reduced state of life. Now I am left wondering again. When I first set out, after watching silent falls of swallows above a cornfield, I found the discredited notion of birds that spent the winter not on the other side of the world but in a reduced state of life. In a long ecstasy between life and death. In a sort of torpor. In the middle state. Science went on to dispose of this notion. Knowledge disproved it. Was science now going on to confirm it? Not in hibernation but in nesting, even in the course of the bird's life. The swift, the most wondrous of them all, the strangest and most unknown, Gilbert White's familiar, his shiftless being, his state of perfection, reducing its metabolic rate until conditions were more favourable. Could the swift be proof that the middle state exists after all?

Before the end of August, when the swallows are still feeding a second or third brood in the sheds, the swifts are gone. They arrive late and they depart early. Swifts do not linger. This is a characteristic of the swift's life in general for whatever space the swift occupies is, in E. M. Nicholson's perfect phrase, 'briefly tenanted'.[11] The swift, as befitting something so airborne, so free of the earth, never stays anywhere for too long. The swift is an itinerant. Living as it does in the air and being so dependent on the vagaries of the weather, the swift is always ready to move on. Cold air means the disappearance of its insect food, means the insect herds have gone elsewhere, means the swift must also move. It moves unceasingly, it moves constantly across the invisible plains of the sky. If the swallow, even the migratory swallow, is, like the sparrow and the jackdaw, a bird of place, a bird of faithful returning to the same ledge and the same nest, the swift is the opposite. The swift is restless, a restlessness that makes the swallow seem sedentary. The swift truly is the shiftless one. Indeed, when it comes to the likes of this farmyard and these fields the swift's connection is purely casual. It is far more common amongst the tall buildings of a town or village. Often, I wondered why the swift was found above the street but not above the field. I wondered why the swift was there and the swallow was here. I was wondering, I was asking, the wrong thing. It is not only that the tall buildings provide high nests for the sky-loving bird but that flying as high as it does and feeding as high as it does, the swift is less affected by aerial pollution and can therefore still thrive in an urban space. So the question should not have been why the swift was there, above the streets, but why the swallow was not. That was where the answer lay. The nature of the city, of the town, means that it is not fit for the swallow. The swift is different. The swift is above all that.

The swift does not belong to those spires and streets, however, the way the swallow belongs to the yard. The territories of the swift, the layers of air, are invisible to us. To confront the idea of place, as this book tries to do, through the perfection of the swift, is to have the notion of place altered beyond any preconceptions held. The swift belongs to invisible places, moves through territories at the boundaries of our imagination, occupies space we can never map. If this book is bordered by a span of walking, cycling miles, is an attempt at exploring the constraints of a bioregion, the swift is this book's antithesis. This book is an attempt at rootedness; the swift flies in the face of that. The restless one knows nothing of my parameters and self-imposed borders. The swift, the alien-looking, high-rise-living urbanite, free of the shackles of place, is the modernist on these pages. As Mark Cocker writes, the swift has no vernacular name now, although it did so in the past. We have no nickname for the mysterious one. Is that simply a sign of our loosening ties with the natural world or is it a sign that the swift just does not belong? The replacement of its old nesting sites with the current ones of tall buildings, church towers and high roofs, seems far more appropriate, as if the swift belongs in those places instead of in old trees or cliffs. A guidebook from 1980 tells me that the older type of nesting sites 'are still being discovered in northern Europe where human habitations are absent'.[12] I do not know if that is still the case but it only adds more to the image that the bird's new sites are an evolutionary niche it has recently discovered. Could it be, after all, that the modernist bird, the alien flyer, the rootless one, the airborne bird living the unimaginable life, has found, like the sparrow and the jackdaw, its proper niche with us.

Like swallows, and unlike most others, the swift migrates during the day. Like the swallows, too, the swift heads towards southern Africa. Somehow, in a bird like the swift, the idea of this migration is not so astonishing. It is the bird itself that is astonishing. The idea that it might fly some 10,000 miles away is hardly unbelievable in a bird that might fly 500 miles a day whilst nesting. It seems even more likely, in the light of this, that Gilbert White's search for hibernating nests was wishful thinking. Such a close observer must have had no trouble believing they flew far, far away. Gilbert White, intrinsic examiner of the particular, would have known the swift's capabilities. He knew how it flew. He knew it went away. He just wished it was not so. In this instance it is not the swift's migration that is the wonder, it is the aspects of migration themselves. As I leaf through guidebooks for information about that stray swift it is the act of migration itself that begins to amaze me. Migratory birds, science now believes, have a star compass and a sun compass. They can read the sky in both ways. They also have the capacity to see what is called polarised light, that is, light that appears in the sky according to the position of the sun, light that cannot be seen by us. Light that emanates even after the sun has set. This is the invisible geography of the migrating swift. It is believed that migrating birds also have a sensitivity to the earth's magnetic fields. Those are the fields of the swift. Those are the pastures of the unknown one. Migrating birds even, in Dominic Couzens' technical and science-rich study *Bird Migration*, have the ability to hear ranges of sound, infrasounds, that push hard against the boundaries of our imagination. 'Can a bird in northern Europe hear the wind disturbances around the Alps and Pyrenees, or hear the rumble of the Mediterranean Sea and Atlantic Ocean?'[13] It seems almost too extraordinary. It seems almost a mistake that a serious study of bird migration, a book of field observation and experimental evidence, should talk of a star compass and invisible polarised light, magnetic fields and infrasounds. If it was not for the evidence of the swift, the incredible fact of its existence, we might think hard science had become wistful. Still when discussing the swift, when describing the act of migration, it is not hard for minds to be challenged. Gilbert White might not have wanted to admit that his flying states of perfection ever left him but many years later close observers were still struggling to come to terms with the reality of the swift. In 1951 E. M. Nicholson was still battling to comprehend the life of the bird so familiar and so essentially singular. 'From the nature of things proof of nights spent in the air is elusive, and it seems an improbable habit, even for so strange a bird.'[14]

For some reason, unlike the peregrine falcon, the swift generates no feelings of removal for me. I do not feel as if it is a bird of the grandstand, a televisual wonder that diminishes the everyday. Perhaps the fact that it is a bird already so removed, a bird that only infrequently strays along a lane or a field, means I have not really identified with it. Instead, I know it as a bird of the town, a bird above the buildings and the traffic, a banal presence in its own way, even though it is in other ways the embodiment of wonder. Yet, it is the simple book-searched categorising of a stray swift that has brought me into an understanding of the incredible. I have heard it said that nature defies categorisation and there is indeed more to the natural world than dry specifics, but the swift is a description of wonder. The bare details of its life are a natural declaration. The bare accountancy of its existence. The false, imagined boundaries I have put on this book, whilst adhering as much as possible to the boundaries of the coast and the contours of hills and fields, have been arbitrarily imposed. Why stop at this field and ignore the next? Why walk this lane but not that? What does nature know of my walking and cycling limits? What bioregion is encompassed by that? The territory I have created does not really exist, it has no natural embodiment. Nature does not accept my definition. Likewise the swift. Whatever can be gleaned by accounting for the simple certainties of its existence, by simply defining it, it eludes definition. How could it not do? How could a bird grazing invisible pastures and building nests from the flotsam of the air do otherwise? How could a bird that leaves the nest as a fledgling and does not return to earth for four years be incorporated by definition? As Mark Cocker writes, we are little less than enchanted by the swift but 'the appeal may possibly rest as much on what we do not know as on their familiarity'.[15] The swift both challenges the extent of our imagination and exists beyond it. To list its characteristics is to be astonished, but those characteristics only pinpoint the limits of our understanding. In that strange way, the distant, alien bird, that is yet so familiar as it flies above our urban streets, is comforting. The swift is a contradiction and our failure to understand it is part of the joy we get from it. Edward Thomas, another English writer embedded in place, recognised just how much the swift could not be understood. 'While over them shrill shrieked in his fierce glee/The swift with wings and tail as sharp and narrow/As if the bow had flown off with the arrow.'[16]

We measure ourselves through our dwellings, recalling our histories through time and the weather.[1]

Jonathan Bate

13

Arguing with an April Wind

Perhaps it is the coming change, the inescapable feeling of the year turning, the pulse of spring that sets my mind wandering. Perhaps it is simply recalling the trapped swift in the hall. Whatever it is, my mind is flitting back to the city these days. Spring has arrived cold and bright, yet the last few days have been wet and the showers have driven even the hardiest indoors. The weather controls so much of what can be done. Outside the backdoor is the shape of the day. It was not always like this, however. Back in the city, back in the days when the swift flew into my sleep, I barely noticed the weather. Even as a backdrop it was largely unimportant. Amongst the tight houses and the streets it often felt as if there was no weather. In the city the weather 'seems hardly to exist. The days are bright, crisp. Occasionally the light lowers or rises, evidence of a cloud passing across the sun somewhere I cannot see it. Life is internal, the weather registered through windows, of houses, of taxis, of buses. When we are outside the weather is unobtrusive. Moving through the canyons of the city, I have no access to the wide sky.'[2]

Now I am scanning the sky and seeing only cold and cloud. The constant rain is in the air. It is getting close to that time when swallows annually appear above the yard but the weather does not feel like swallow weather. Spring is out there but it is out there somewhere: somewhere in the waking trees and the movement of birds and animals in the fields. It is there in the pond and in the soil, in the insects. It is simply that I cannot see it. They used to call this, still do no doubt in parts of this island, *Laethanta na Bó Riabhaí*, from an old legend about a cow that complained about the weather. *Laethanta na Bó Riabhaí* are these early days of April borrowed from March, days that still have March's cold and rain. These are the days we are in now. Looking out I cannot help thinking about a culture that lay so close to nature it even had a myth for a few days at the beginning of April. I am back again amongst the division we cannot avoid, between the culture of our past and the culture we now have, the one time culture of our relationship with nature and the culture of that relationship today, the culture of an Irish language and the culture without that language. I know I have read about this feeling somewhere and I turn away from the cold outside the window and look it up.

'There would appear to be a conflict of sentiment here between the modern scientific names of nature and those who cherish the older relationship with nature represented by the Gaelic vernacular . . . the Gaelic names for plants and animals express a primitive community living from the land and the sea, intimate with seasonal cycles and alert to the aspects of the natural world that were beneficial or detrimental to themselves, whereas the Latin scientific names for obscure or unappealing plant and animal groups seem to lead no further than the taxonomist's laboratory.'[3] There is a harshness there with which I cannot completely concur. Irish language description of even one species of bird was, as I have already discovered, so rich, so diverse that it did not necessarily create the grounds for an understandable dissemination of knowledge. I cannot think of J. P. Burkitt ringing the legs of robins in his back garden in Fermanagh, or Ellen Hutchins examining moss in the damp corners of Bantry and think that their intimacy with nature lead only towards taxonomy, that they were estranged from their environment. Still, the days of the Gaelic vernacular hardly had a relationship with the weather that consisted of a forecast on the television. I sit and remember the city. I gaze out of the window. Even if it is cold and the rain is always threatening, I think, I'll put on a coat and go out and walk in it. I can search for swallows.

If the city can sometimes feel as if it has no weather the Irish countryside often feels as if it has an awful lot. A walk in the rain can quite easily end as a stroll in the sunshine. Rain segues into sunshine into rain and back again. A description of Ireland excluding the weather would be like sitting down to a meal without tasting it. Chet Raymo, writing on the Dingle Peninsula not a million miles away from here, noted that it was 'not unusual for two fronts to pass over the country in a single day. A day that begins in mist and drizzle can end in brilliant sunshine. A day that begins calm and bright can end with a gale. And the only way to tell what the weather will be like tomorrow is to look out of the window when you wake up.'[4] Wandering on from that, Chet Raymo also states, when recounting an American man who made a close study of the shape of snowflakes, that 'all that we know, now and forever, all scientific knowledge that we have of this world, or will ever have, is an island in the sea'.[5] The Irish weather appears to have led him on to this, the constant variation of environment that it provides. The unsteady, unpredictable nature of it. Walking the fields and lanes of a small corner of an Irish peninsula led him to appreciate the limits and boundaries of human knowledge, the epistemological borders that nature provides for us. Criss-crossing beneath the clouds and the blue sky. Hearing the silence of a still day or standing in the face of a coming storm. It is probably worth noting in this instance that the man acknowledging and revelling in this sense of mystery and wonder, this ceiling to knowing, was a Professor of Physics and Astronomy.

The weather is always the great reminder of living in the wider environment of a planet and even for those living or writing about a particular bioregion there is the realisation, as the sun shines or the storm breaks, that our weather knows nothing at all of our imposed boundaries, our limitations. Ireland's weather streams in from the Atlantic. Out there. I face south for a moment, although fully aware that the Atlantic fronts move in from the west and north too. So I turn around and look north over the gap in the trees and see the slope of the land and the rise on the far side above the river. Out there, where the railway used to be and where we so often see rain approaching, and know it is coming before a drop has fallen. Far out over the North Atlantic cool air from the Arctic and tropical air from Bermuda are in something approaching constant conflict. As Brendan McWilliams, another to have revelled in the unending vagaries of our weather, recorded, 'the weather systems that affect Ireland today may have originated hundreds, or even thousands of miles away a day or two ago'.[6] I glance up at the sky as I think of that. I look up at the clouds. I think of the air as I breathe it in. I put my hand out to the rain. I wonder how many miles away it might have originated or who else's hands it has brushed past. I walk on and take a short shelter beneath some tall sycamores. A flurry of crows and a woodpigeon break away from nearby and sound as they leave as if they are falling down the stairs. Within a short time the rain has eased and the sun has appeared. I smile at this on-cue behaviour of the weather. It is as if the 'miniature dramas' and 'sense of theatre'[7] of the Irish climate cannot be put in abeyance. The incessant change, from day to day, from hour to hour. The turbulent mix that fundamentally dictates our climate, the cold air moving south and the warm air moving north, all taking place out there over the North Atlantic, does it ever stop?

Pitting scientific study against folklore one contemporary ornithologist has felt moved enough to describe most beliefs about bird behaviour and the weather as not only false but, in at least one case, as 'palpable nonsense'.[8] Bird movement does not predict the weather, we are reassured, it responds to it. The swifts fly around the weather front because of its arrival not with foreknowledge of it. The swallows delay their arrival because of the bad weather in front of them not because they know it is arriving. Somehow this interpretation itself appears to signify a gap between experience of the environment and the recording of it. It is assessing bird behaviour and the natural patterns of the environment at such a remove as to lose sight of how we ourselves experience both the birds themselves and the face of the weather. Quite simply, saying that the birds react to the weather rather than in advance of it is, standing on a lane or walking through a field, more or less the same thing. Our vision is limited, by and large, to close movements around us. Unless we inhabit or daily visit areas with a wide vantage we look out at the yard, go as far as the lane, glance up at the field, peer through the gap in the hedgerow. Birds, by contrast, are quite often responding to weather we cannot yet see. Their vision, in many common species, is far less limited than ours. Their sudden movements, their gatherings or departures, if we are not sitting in the study or examining records of their behaviour, if we are standing in the backyard, may well be the first inkling we could have of approaching weather. We may not recognise the movements as such but that does not mean the patterns are not there. It is certainly no stretch of the imagination or attempt to use folklore as a cover for ignorance to suggest that others on this island who lived lives far more entwined with nature, through necessity as much as anything else, might have been far better at observing those passing patterns than we are. Our interpretation of that behaviour, our assessment, may well say as much about our culture as it does the phenomena we are observing. Writing, this time specifically of the snowflake and the wonderfully close observations one individual made of it, Chet Raymo begins to suggest that this example of our weather, rare enough as it is in this country, is both an 'emblem of order' and an 'insignia of disorder' and that it is this 'kaleidoscopic balance of order and disorder that is the basis for all beauty in art and in nature'.[9] The snowflake aside, this could quite easily be applied to the Irish weather itself. It is both chaotic and perfectly still, all within moments. There is much truth, too, in the assertion that art and nature are difficult to divide. That has been one of the experiences of this book, this walk between field and book, lane and page. Like all of the artificial divisions we place around our knowledge, be it dividing history from literature or biology from geography, however useful they might be, it is the recognition that they are false that can often let us see more clearly. Simon Schama's belief that without culture there was no nature was merely to impose boundaries where there were not any. The idea of a hermetically sealed culture is broken if you feel the rain on your face. The weather, the everyday air outside our backdoors, is enough to remind us of that. Whether it is thought of or not, the Irish rain will surely fall. In writing this book I have passed backwards and forwards between nature and literature, between direct experience and recorded encounter. True, I have sought out and believe nature itself to be the source. Whatever words can be written about a blackbird's song or a swallow's flight they are as nothing if you have never heard or seen those things for yourself. I can write about the Irish rain but standing beneath it or merely watching it fall is the simplest truth of it. That said, I have struggled most of the time to establish a true demarcation between the literature I have discovered and the nature that has inspired it. I have found early monastic simplicities on the song of the blackbird which have brought me as close to that noise as hearing it in the yard. I have found Ellen Hutchin's accounts of her delving in the damp places of Bantry to have been as real as walking through a sodden corner. I have found Robert Lloyd Praeger's account of walking across Ireland as revealing as walking these lanes myself. The words have brought me as close as is hard to delineate to the moment itself. Always finding company has left me feeling the difference between the literature and the song as something never finely defined. Of course art and nature are different. That is their essence. But they are not quite as separate as might first seem. Even the arch-modernist and often disturbed thinker Ezra Pound, one of the leading lights of an art that sought to shake off the shackles of place, could not escape the most immediate and obvious example of what lay outside the backdoor when attempting to explain his aesthetic. 'Beauty in art reminds one what is worth while. I am not now speaking of shams. I mean beauty, not slither, not sentimentalising about beauty, not telling people that beauty is the proper and respectable thing. I mean beauty. You don't argue about an April wind.'[10] Even, it seems, debating the very nature of art there is an unavoidable resource to the most obvious physicality of the natural world: the form of the weather. Another leading art critic, John Ruskin, who also happened to be an enthusiastic meteorologist when study of the weather was gaining momentum, recognised the immediacy of the natural world as a source of wonder and intellectual delight.

'He whose kingdom is the heavens can never meet with an uninteresting space or exhaust the phenomena of an hour; he is in a realm of perpetual change, of eternal motion, of infinite mystery. Light and darkness, cold and heat, are all to him as friends of familiar countenance but of infinite variety of conversation; and while the geologist yearns for the mountain, the botanist for the field, and the mathematician for the study, the meteorologist is a spirit of a higher order than any, and rejoices in the kingdom of the air.'[11]

The phenomena of an hour. A realm of perpetual change. A source of infinite variety of conversation. I do not know if John Ruskin ever visited Ireland but he certainly captured the Irish weather. Between the words and the rain it is hard to see the join.

Whatever of John Ruskin, there were here in Ireland individuals who actively sought to capture the Irish weather. Even when we simply face into the wind or watch the rain there is, as always, company. An English doctor, John Rutty, moved to Dublin in 1724 and promptly set about keeping detailed weather records for the next fifty years. From Rutty's own carefully compiled daily observations and data from other weather diaries to which he had access at the time, the result is a comprehensive and detailed pen-picture of Irish weather from 1716 to 1766. Each day looking out at the rain and the sun. Standing beneath the showers. Feeling on his face the weather that had originated hundreds or thousands of miles away. Richard Kirwan, too, born in Galway in 1733, turned his face towards the weather. Using barometers, thermometers, and a rain gauge he made himself, for over twenty years he detailed the weather from the garden of his house in Dublin. He went out into his backyard and found a lifetime's fascination in the very shape of the day. Of course, for every one of these individuals who left a record of their thoughts and their knowledge, there are the many thousands and thousands who simply experienced the weather as the rudimentary reality of their days. For them, there was never a day when the weather did not exist.

I have no intention of arguing with an April wind yet during these days of cold and rain I am scanning the skies ever more closely. As I watch the clouds bank up across the fields I imagine that even now the swallows from this yard are waiting to cross over, held up by unfavourable weather. If it is our national pastime to complain about the weather, today I am joining in. 'I'm afraid it must be a chronic affliction. Every year I fret away the damp and birdless days of early April, wondering if they will ever come back,'[12] wrote Richard Mabey and these days most of all, I understand what he meant. There is still a fire lit in the house now in the evening, but the temperature is not really going to affect the movement of the birds, unless of course it is the extremes of something, like the Sahara that the yard-born, day-migrating swallows will already have crossed by night in order to avoid the heat. No, it is after all the April wind that could be delaying them. It may even have caused them to turn back. If they had set out and were then confronted not just by rain but by facing winds or crosswinds, that might have been enough to send them back again. Ornithologists call it reverse migration. Thankfully, it is only a temporary measure. They will be waiting. I am waiting. The borrowed days of March in early April, the rain and the wind, I watch them through the window. I walk in them. I stand in the doorway of an outhouse in the yard and watch them, look up, scanning the skies.

In his account of intensive wandering over this island Robert Lloyd Praeger saw fit to commence his description of the way that he went with a description of the climate. It was for him, who had experienced it at first hand in all its manifestations, something that was forever 'intruding itself strikingly in Ireland' and had an effect upon 'all life within the island, from man down to mosses'.[13] From man down to mosses. In Ireland, out here in the Atlantic, it has been ever thus. Frank Mitchell, writing of a deteriorating climate towards the end of the Bronze Age, describes an Ireland we would all too readily recognise. 'Waterlogged and ruined crops . . . rivers bursting their banks and weeks of leaden skies and unceasing rain. Ireland's late Bronze Age farmers, soaked, cold and hungry, could have felt themselves on the brink of Armageddon. We all know the feeling.'[14] The weather can be said, in fact, to have played more than just an everyday role in the history of this country. Theobald Wolfe Tone, for instance, had no doubt about the part the climate played in his attempts at an uprising. Writing of his days aboard a French frigate in Bantry Bay, waiting to invade and spark a rebellion in his home country in 1796, he wrote: 'notwithstanding all our blunders, it is the dreadful stormy weather and the easterly winds, which have been blowing furiously and without intermission since we made Bantry Bay, that have ruined us.'[15]

Likewise the catastrophic events of the Great Famine, political and social factors aside, owe much to the warm, wet weather that gave rise to the initial blight:

On continental Europe and in Britain the summer of 1846 was dry and hot, and so the blight died out, but the Irish weather collaborated cruelly. From late July onwards, just when the all-important potato plants were reaching their maturity, it was abnormally wet and warm. The first sign of the resurgent disease was a pervasive, tell-tale stench of decay which permeated the air even when the stalks remained deceptively luxuriant; it was followed by livid patches on the leaves, which advanced until the stem became a putrid mass; by early August the fields were black with rotting plants and the season's crop was an almost total loss.[16]

The following year it was again the weather that impacted upon a now weakened population. As one voice born with living memory of those times recalled, 'the year which was called Black Forty Seven came with rain and snow and frost and the cold was fierce. The weather was so bad that they thought no crops or potatoes would grow.'[17] Such was the immediate experience of the environment in that Ireland that bad weather could and did mean death.

This intrinsic relationship with the environment, and with the obvious manifestation of nature that is the climate, reinforces the culture that related such things as bird behaviour to the weather. There were stories about robins and cuckoos and the weather, and a flight of swallows, for example, was invariably a sign of rain, *is tuar fearthainne ealt ainleog*. Again, whatever angle scientific studies of bird behaviour adopt, and I am not for one moment questioning the veracity of their findings, I sense an obvious truth in those prosaic observations. If this behaviour was being observed by people used to being outside, used to collecting clues from their close, daily environment, the first sign they might get of an approaching weather front would be from movements in the natural world, of which bird behaviour would be an obvious example. In particular with the swallows, the internal movements across field and ditch of an air-dependent species as an indicator of incoming weather seems to make complete sense. Crows, jackdaws, gulls, swallows, pigeons, flocks of finches, sparrows, starlings all move across this yard and above the trees and along the fields in patterns of flight and behaviour I often do not understand. Perhaps if I was tied to an outdoor life more I would do, perhaps I would know from experience what certain movements of birds meant, perhaps I would conclude that a particular flight of swallows meant particular weather was imminent. After all, as I wait these days, I am aware that climatic conditions are bound up in their arrival, as they will be months hence in their departure. I stand in the doorway of an outbuilding that is stocked with winter wood and the sunlight falls into the space behind me. The arbitrary nature of the time divisions we impose on the outside world and nature are never more evident than on days like these. The calendar may say one thing but the passage of the seasons does not necessarily correspond. Changes wrought by global warming – a looming presence for us all – notwithstanding, the idea that we have a calendar day that declares summer has begun or summer has ended does not appear to bear much resemblance to physical reality. Standing in this doorway on a cold April morning I can only go by the immediacy of my senses. Blue tits, like the ones that nest in the box attached to the huge, old ash tree, time the arrival of their chicks to coincide with the arrival of particular insects. It is deemed likely that global warming will disrupt the closely timed nature of that relationship and as an indicator of damage wrought by a shift in temperature it is an alarming signal. It also denotes, though, how bird behaviour and bird movement are far more accurate indicators of climate conditions than some might lead us to believe. Standing here in the yard, from the angle of this old doorway, a predictive relationship between bird movements and the weather does not seem like palpable nonsense to me. I am not suggesting the birds are doing anything but responding to the weather, it just depends upon where you're standing as to how you view that behaviour.

Somewhere out there, out over the sea, waiting for this weather to break, birds born in this concrete yard have come back over the Sahara, over the rainforests of the Congo. Responding to barometric pressure or thermal currents they are feeding on airborne insects, low in the sky or high, depending on which conditions exist. 'Of the five or six offspring of a typical adult pair, only one is likely to survive the journey to return the following year.'[18] I take myself out to experience the weather. The sunshine, the scudding clouds, the rain, the tropical-like showers, the song of the wind, the sky, the true atmosphere of the world. The April wind. If only one summer bird is likely to make it back, the least I can do is be here to salute it.

The strivings of the imagination must be reconciled with connection to the earth.[1]

Jonathan Bate

14

As Much About Books

I did not for one moment believe, when I first set out, that I would ever come to fully know that field above my house, or this yard outside my backdoor, or the lane leading down to the straight road, or the myriad of other lanes and fields that have contributed to the geography of this book. There are so many strands to a history that it would have taken a far more magisterial work than this to achieve that. All I hoped for was that by the end, by the days that my expectant gaze was turning towards the sky again, that I would have gleaned and kept some knowledge. All I wanted was an understanding. I am nearly there now and the swallows will, I trust, soon return. I will soon be back at the beginning. I am not sure, as I wait, whether I have truly got under the skin of this place, whether I dwell here any more deeply than previously, but I do feel some kind of heightened awareness. Rightly or wrongly, I do. Nature, looking more intensely at nature, has given me that. And art has given it to me too. Every step I have taken, I have taken in the company of somebody else. I did not realise that would be the case when I first set out but this has been as much about books as it has about gorse or seals, blackbirds or swifts. Everything I have seen has made me look somewhere else. Each looking out has made me look in.

Of course, I write all of this from a distance. As an outsider. I am not from here and I did not really grow up here. Whilst that distance is relevant on a personal level, the personal element to this story is not of any great import; that condition, that distance, is something that is not unique. True, the very act of this book is a distance, a stepping back, but art itself is like that and the condition of us all is like that. How many of us, especially in the western world, how many of us inhabit a place without that distance? Seamus Heaney wrote that there are two ways in which a place can be known. 'One is lived, illiterate and unconscious, the other learned, literate and conscious.'[2] The illiterate in that sense is not meant in any kind of pejorative way but as a recognition that that kind of way of inhabiting a space, of belonging, is lost to most of us. So, while I may well have written here about belonging because I do not, that is not simply a personal experience. Giraldus Cambrensis, J. P. Burkitt, Richard Ussher, Ellen Hutchins, David Thomson, Mary Carbery, even Roderic O'Flaherty estranged by the loss of his land, even Seamus Heaney from one side of a border, they are all outsiders too and whilst there may be something there about the particularities of an Irish relationship and specifically an Irish relationship with nature, that estrangement is not confined by an Irish situation any more than it is by my personal situation. Seamus Heaney, again, writing about the wonders of the early Irish nature poetry that walked with me in this book, noted that the 'tang and clarity of a pristine world full of woods and water and birdsong seems to be present in the words. Little jabs of delight in the elemental . . .'[3] Those poems, the words within them, have a sense of biological dwelling. They belong, and they belong almost unconsciously, however much they are art. The truth remains, however, that for all the beauty and immediacy of that early poetry, the pristine world – the world of woods and water and birdsong – is lost to us. That lack of distance, that ease of inhabitation, is gone. The poetry itself gives voice to that. The tang and the clarity are the taste of what is missing.

Not that I believe anything but nature itself should be the first port of call. To experience a tree you have to stand beneath a tree. To feel the water you have to stand in the river. To see a swallow you have to face into the sky. If there is some kind of crude palimpsest of the landscape it is the physical, material reality that is the first layer. The poem does not create the blackbird. It may well create our consciousness of it, may well reflect our learning more than our direct experience, may hopefully even enhance our seeing of it, but the blackbird is still the source. Whatever poetry signifies, whatever art speaks of, without the blackbird there is none. Through the terrain of Simon Schama's landscape, the landscape that is a work of the mind, we may well lug our 'heavy cultural backpacks'[4] – this book itself is a testament to that. Perhaps it is true too, as this book also attests, that humanity's impact upon the land in the context of culture, as opposed to the grim ecological accounting we might usually find ourselves in, is more often than not a 'cause not for guilt and sorrow but celebration'.[5] I would hope to have illustrated clearly that my pleasure in walking a lane or watching an otter has been enhanced by those whose written work has kept me company. Those who have walked before me; who went their way before I went mine. My heavy cultural backpack was never a burden. I have sought to celebrate them all. From those margin-scribbling monks to the damp meanderings of Ellen Hutchins, from David Thomson through to Simon Schama himself, for his faith in our 'tough, lovely old planet'.[6] If it is true that it is 'our shaping perception that makes the difference between raw matter and landscape',[7] there is still the material reality of the raw matter. Before the demesne, before the trees of the planter, there was the forest. Before the whistle of the bright yellow-billed little bird, there is the blackbird itself. In a world where experience of nature is defined by removal, by a sense of separateness, by a lack of belonging, it is the footstep on the lane that has to be the first contact. Patrick Duffy commences his touchstone exploration of the Irish landscape by noting that for many people today, 'cyber worlds are more familiar than the local material landscape'.[8] Opening the backdoor might well be the first response to that. It is better to see the swallows depart before discovering what others have thought of that. Better still to see them arrive. Then the repositories of culture and the gifts of shared memory can be most fruitfully enjoyed. It is not that the book as an object is inferior but that the worth of it is best appreciated if the song it describes has been heard. Beyond that, nature and culture go hand in hand. Standing in the yard is one thing. Standing in the yard having read the words of all the others is something else. Appreciation of a poem about the blackbird's song is hardly likely to be unaccompanied by an appreciation of the song itself. Nature and culture are in this together, even if, as with Patrick Duffy's cyber familiars, they also face their colonisers. 'The world of culture and nature, which is actual, is almost a shadow world now, and the insubstantial world of political jurisdictions and rarefied economies is what passes for reality.'[9]

As I have admitted, by the simple act of this book I am distancing myself. The performance of writing is in itself an enactment of distance; it comes out of that and is realised by that. It carries with it an acknowledgement of loss. It flags the distance. I have used the words and interpretations of others so much because I believed that through them I could imagine the lost forests and the vast bogs. I believed that through them I might find a way into a clearer hearing of the blackbird's song or understand the silent swallows above the cornfield. That the words might lead me into the clearing. In truth though, a little like a childhood, most of what I searched for is already gone. The bypass runs beside the cornfield far more insistently than the middle state of a swallow. For every time I stand in the backyard and hear the blackbird sing there is a time when I stand and hear the rumble of traffic. Looking, seeking to belong or even understand belonging, I realise I have used art to find my way home and in doing so I have stumbled into the contradictions that are inherit in the relationship between nature and culture. Art is both the 'attempt to recover the very thing which has been destroyed so that art can be made'[10] and 'the place of exile where we grieve for our lost home upon the earth'.[11] Those who are still fully inhabiting a place, who live in a place without the necessity of explanation, do not require the artist. Those who know the true names of the fields do not need interpretations. In reality though, across the globe, they must be increasingly few in number. For most of us culture is our shelter. True, the very fact of art is a sign that the forests are lost and the vast wetlands drained. That is why art exists. That is why the monks wrote, that is why the Gaelic poets sang of their lost society, why David Thomson wrote that he stood on the cusp of a dying culture. Art cannot do anything about that. It cannot change that. Yet, while the distance cannot be erased, the length of it can be reduced. Delving into the words of those before me I hoped to get closer. 'The presence of memory means that the countryside is inhabited rather than viewed aesthetically,'[12] Jonathan Bate wrote. I mined the memories. I took the farmer's names for his fields and Roderic O'Flaherty's words for the gannet diving and I sought there for a place upon the earth. I looked into the writings and with them took a few steps more. I came upon what was, in effect, another contradiction, a joyous contradiction, in that the place of exile, the attempt to recover, the work of art, the poem or the writing, could in itself be an experience of nature. An artificial one, yes, a representation say, rather than a walk through ancient woodland. That does not, however, make it unreal. The pristine world is in those poems. We can sense it through them. We can feel the tang and the clarity, the elemental. I can almost walk through those vast and untamed lakes, rivers and marshes since I read Gordon D'Arcy's book. I can see them. I can see the teeming flock of goldfinches since William Cobbett. I can hear the silence for miles along the moist fields, the whole length and breadth of Ireland, since Seán Ó Faoláin. In the way that a city park is artificial and a representation but still a very true, authentic experience, those writings are an experience of nature too. In an Irish context the lost forests are perhaps the most fundamental characteristic of the landscape but the tree-rich demesnes that replaced them, however biologically inauthentic they might be, are genuine Irish environments too. Where W. B. Yeats meditated upon a swallow's flight at Lady Gregory's Coole Park estate, he wrote that 'Under my window-ledge the waters race/Otters below and moor-hens on the top,/Run for a mile undimmed in Heaven's face'.[13] Otters and moor-hens and the racing water. That does not sound artificial, neither the demesne nor the poem. Nature and culture, one certainly precedes the other, but I often have trouble telling the difference.

Still, nature is the starting point. The earth itself. In celebrating it, there can be nothing to be gained from not giving a truthful account. There is no point in denying the state of the environment. There would have been no point in opening the backdoor if I were to deliberately avoid seeing what is potentially so devastating. Science is approaching unanimity about the parlous state of the natural world. There is a consensus now about the state we are in. Natural loss is not something belonging to the past. The vanished pristine world is not merely indicative of an environmental deficit that is centuries old. It is here with us now. It is our world today. It is where we are. It is outside the window, outside the backdoor. Those enduring weather patterns over the North Atlantic may well be changing. Global warming is here. What will that mean for those gatherings of swallows, for those screaming swifts? The things lost, the huge environmental changes that I encountered along the way, are a part of this story now and not just historical curios. They were not included out of a sense of melancholy but because, even though many of them are gone, they are a part of the full picture. Those lost forests are part of what has brought us to where we are today and where we are today we will somehow have to live with.

The flowing cars going east and west. The names of the fields. The old address of a townland. The ice-age contours disappearing beneath earth-moving machinery. The unchanging order of things that was the incessant call of the corncrake. The long ecstasy of the middle-state swallows. The unmapped desire paths. The lost, young men and women of the 1950s. The humble cabins of a townland. The landscape amnesia. The lazy beds. The tide gone out for good on the thirty-one words for seaweed. The many names for the lingering, playful, chough. *Inis na bhfiodhbhadh.* The island of woods. The lost forests. The elemental simplicity. The majesty and silence of the primeval wood. *Tá deireadh na gcoillte ar lár.* The last of the woods laid low. The woodkerne and the wolf. The sauntering. The black streams and the secret pools of water. The particularities of place. The labourers and the cottiers. The flock of 10,000 goldfinches. The huge bonfires of DDT birds. The 500 million slaughtered on the American plains. The 140 or so remaining grey partridge. The darnel and the fat hen, the corn cockle and the corn marigold. The idea of a sacredness in the land. The monk sitting before a wall of forest. The great, vast and untamed estuaries and lagoons. The wetlands and the black lakes. The forgotten landscape. The unsophisticated spot and the otter of memory. The roots of the bog going back 10,000 years. The raven and the myth and the legend. The Donegal rock 1.7 billion years old. Being on good terms with the seals. The huge shoals of starlings above the neon signs. The declining common sparrow. The little parcels of the enclosures. The stock-in-trade of an Irish speaker's mind. The things founded clean on their own shapes. The common occurrences, the shiftless beings and the state of perfection. The intimacy with the seasonal cycles. 'The old dens are soaking./The pads are lost or/Retrieved by small vermin/That glisten and scut./Nothing is panting, lolling,/Vapouring. The tongue's/Leashed in my throat.'[14]

Rachel Carson's peerless *Silent Spring*, despite the hostile power of the press and the chemical industry, exposed for the whole world the horrific consequences of an earlier ecological threat. She was dismissed as 'an hysterical woman', as being too literate to have scientific credibility, and as being 'more poisonous than the pesticides she condemns'.[15] Indeed, it was only in 1963, just a year before Rachel Carson died, that the

United States authorities admitted that 'until the publication of *Silent Spring*, people were generally unaware of the toxicity of pesticides'.[16] Less than fifty years ago powerful concerns, respected and admired corporations, were able to inflict devastating environmental damage simply because nobody knew. Rachel Carson's book, her science and her literature, her art, awoke the world to the truth of pesticides as a farming tool. Reading it now, with the awareness of our current ecological frailty, is to sense still the immediacy of her concerns. 'Over increasingly large areas of the United States, spring now comes unheralded by the return of the birds, and the early mornings are strangely silent where once they were filled with the beauty of bird song. This sudden silencing of the song of birds, this obliteration of the colour and beauty and interest they lend to our world has come about swiftly, insidiously, and unnoticed by those whose communities are as yet unaffected.'[17] Suddenly, swiftly, insidiously and unnoticed. Common bird populations collapsing quickly because of insecticide spraying. In some cases, virtually disappearing. It is not possible to walk a locality, to have a small radius of hills and cliffs and fields as the nucleus of discovery without realising that the hill beyond, the lane over there and the next stretch of cliff-side are part of the story too. 'Neither ecosystems nor social customs are co-extensive with national boundaries; acid rain and nuclear fallout do not respect the lines that are drawn on human maps.'[18] It is not possible to watch the simple delight of the swallow's flight without reflecting upon the environmental state of the world they inhabit, the state of all the different land they fly above. Swallows were present, too, in Rachel Carson's work. When she describes 'summer mornings without bird song' she notes of swallows 'that cruise the skies, straining out the aerial insects as herring strain the plankton of the sea' that they have been 'hard hit. Everyone complains of how few they have compared to four or five years ago. Our sky overhead was full of them only four years ago. Now we seldom see any . . .'[19] Walking the earth or thinking on the lane cannot be done without reflecting on the state of nature. There is always company and sometimes that company has a stark message and always that company has words, words that may have been written years ago, but still carry the truth within them today.

'Who has made the decision that sets in motion these chains of poisonings, this ever-widening wave of death that spreads out, like ripples when a pebble is dropped into a still pond? Who has placed in one pan of the scales the leaves that might have been eaten by the beetles and in the other the pitiful heaps of many-hued feathers, the lifeless remains of the birds that fell before the unselective bludgeon of insecticide poisons? Who has decided, who has the right to decide for the countless legions of people who were not consulted, that the supreme value is a world without insects, even though it also would be a sterile world ungraced by the curving wing of a bird in flight. The decision is that of the authoritarian temporarily entrusted with power; he has made it during a moment of inattention by millions to whom beauty and the ordered world of nature still have a meaning that is deep and imperative.'[20]

If art is the guide, the parallel path, those written words, the letters and poems, memories and accounts, nature is still the core and nature, however close I may get, remains apart. The difference is always there. 'As an indeterminate something, natural beauty is hostile to all definition.'[21] Nature brings me always back to the blurred boundaries and the limits of understanding. It is a challenge to our presumed hegemony. A reminder. A comfort. There is an undeniable beauty in the universe of Linnaeus, amongst the works of Hutchins and Burkitt, all that gorgeous ordering. It has given us so much. Nature, however, continues to be what eludes us. Nature escapes. However much we net it, it slips through the hands of art. Outside the backdoor is again enough of a reminder of that. In winter, at the bird table by the ditch, the greenfinch is dominant. An ever present, angry-looking visage, always at the feeder. Other species wait their turn but the greenfinch dominates. Then, summer comes and the greenfinch melts away. It goes from being the dominant species to barely visible. Right there, yards from the backdoor, some movement in nature that I know nothing about. Are the greenfinches following some kind of what ornithologists call a pattern of dispersal? Some set of small, limited movements that I am only dimly aware of, that I do not really see? Much like the gulls that pass over from time to time. Going where? Why? Like the flocks of bramblings that noisily descend upon the hedgerow trees for a few weeks and then are gone. Arriving from where? Leaving for where? Like the redwings and fieldfares that appear overnight in a cold field. Coming and going.

At the end of last summer, a September evening with a red sky in the west, I went out into the yard and in the fading warmth the sky around was full of moving birds. Flocks of crows moved across the field while another black flock moved in the opposite direction above the house. There was clearly a purpose to these movements, clearly a pattern, but I had no idea what it could be. A flock of sparrows broke noisily from time to time from the ditch, reappeared against the house, in the dust of the yard, and then scattered again back into the greenery. They were wandering with no clear destination and no defined purpose. They were meandering as new, young birds will do. Sauntering. And then, of course, there were the swallows, swirling their unbordered patterns. More than forty restless swallows flying on and off the roof of the house as I watched. At times some of them left and flew away before coming back. At other times all of them would fly up and away. I had no idea what all of these bird movements constituted. Just outside my backdoor, in the sky above the house and in the hedgerow that borders the acre, a commerce of birds of which I had no understanding. Of course, there are birds coming and going across the Irish skies throughout the year. By March summer migrants are arriving and continue to do so as the season goes on. By July fledglings have left the nest and are dispersing away from their nest sites. By August some of the summer migrants are commencing their return journey and throughout September and October huge numbers of these migrants are departing. Over the rest of the winter, winter migrants are washing up here, escaping more adverse conditions elsewhere. By March the whole thing commences again. That is the framework. That is what is known. It is the skeleton of a body of movement that I cannot pinpoint. Out there, watching the birds flying here and moving there, I realise there is a pulse to the landscape I only barely detect and an unseen geography for which I have a very poor map. I am again at the borders of my understanding.

In David Thomson's *The People of the Sea*, his journey through the sea and seal culture of Scotland and the western coast of Ireland, he writes of a society with 'no direct cultural link with the past',[22] of a society feeling self-conscious about tradition. He was writing about the Ireland of the late 1940s. Sixty years later are we, too, without a cultural link with the past, are we self-conscious about tradition? Sixty years later, what is our link with the cultures of the past and what is our relationship with the natural world? Where is the relationship that was an inherent part of past lives? What is this new country we inhabit like? In the novelty of the moment it often appears as if the past is either dismissed or bathed in nostalgia. A preceding decade is the cause for televisual reminiscence but any integral link with past, with the past as a layer of what we have now, has more or less vanished. The natural world is now something packaged for an hour's spectacular entertainment or something that is the preserve of an exotic holiday. Our relationship with it seems to be at more of a distance than ever. The intensity of the culture Thomson uncovered is unknown to us. The idea that curiosity or phenomena could be found outside the backdoor is not considered. The link, the accepted, unconsidered link with the ordinary, the immediate, the close, has gone.

The modernist poet Basil Bunting was in many ways a literary contradiction. He was part of a movement that saw itself as urban and metropolitan, free of the constraints of place and free of the traditions of form. Free of the past. The modernists were distinctly cosmopolitan. Yet Basil Bunting was also rooted in his Northumbrian home and in that way he found himself writing of a closeness to place that inevitably led him to a consideration of the natural world. He wrote of a nature that is composed of 'things beautiful but hard to define, and it opposes the sharp sun that wants all things to be chained to the dictionary or the multiplication table. It gives not so much tolerance as enthusiastic acceptance of a world in which things are not measured by their usefulness to man'.[23] Nature is not only the thing that slips out of the tightly controlled columns of the recording ledger, the thing that appears in the margins of a monk's manuscript, it is apart from us even when we live close to it. We can live in it, be even a part of it, share its rhythms and its patterns but we cannot define it. It will always be outside of the limits of our understanding and it will always be beyond the limits of our representation. Our relationship with the earth must include the acceptance that there is a border to our art and our science but there is no restriction to our wonder. We can also realise that what we have lost is still there. Outside the backdoor there is still the earth.

I have tried, setting out from the backdoor, to get close to an understanding of this. Sometimes my understanding has felt clear and bright; other times, and perhaps my writing has unfortunately reflected this, it has felt confused and overwhelmed. I have had to come to terms with these limits to art and science and not only recognise them but, as Basil Bunting said, enthusiastically accept them. Strangely enough, I have realised that the acceptance has in many ways brought me closer to a true realisation of the earth around me. I have still watched the movement of the birds without having to know exactly what that movement means. It has been true, too, even though I did not start off from that place, that opening the backdoor has also meant reflecting upon nature and the past. However much I have not thought it was, have not wanted it to be, some of this journey has been a reaction against a society that seems determined to live at a distance from its environment, that seems to revel in it, that seems to see it as a destination. The poet Rainer Maria Rilke, again writing at a time that had not yet in any way reached our levels of virtual and cyber detachment wrote of previous societies that ' a "house", a "well", a familiar tower, their very clothes, their coat: were infinitely more, infinitely more intimate: almost everything a vessel in which they found the human and added to the store of the human . . . We are perhaps the last to still have known such things.'[24] Are we the last, again?

Writing in 1892 the ornithologist Charles Dixon was still

open to the idea that some swallows may hibernate. Whilst accepting that the majority migrate he sees no reason not to believe that some at least may well remain in a state where 'vital functions are partially arrested, animation is suspended, and a death-like trance or stupor, a lethargic sleep, eventually supervenes'.[25] To support this description of the middle state he reaches back over the centuries and describes a number of various accounts.

> In 1666 Schefferus records in the Philosophical Transactions, that swallows sink into lakes in autumn, and hibernate in a manner precisely similar to frogs. In 1741, Fermier-Général Witkowski made legal testimony to the effect that two swallows had been taken from a pond at Didlaeken in his presence, in a torpid state; that they eventually regained animation, and after fluttering about, died some three hours after their capture. In 1748, the great Swedish chemist Wallerius, wrote that he had on several occasions seen swallows clustering on a reed, until they all disappeared beneath the surface. In 1750, Kalm the traveller observed swallows on the 10th of April, sitting on posts near the sea, with their plumage wet as though they had just emerged from the water. Four years later J. R. Foster (editor of Kalm's *Travels in North America*) was an eye-witness, so he informs us, to the following. In January 1754, several swallows were taken from the lake of Lybshau, then covered with ice, one of which he carried home, where it regained its vitality, but died soon afterwards.[26]

How is it that over 200 years later when we know these accounts to be misguided we are, all the same, actually further away from the swallow than ever before? In truth a bird such as the swallow, a bird so immediate and so insistent in its existence, is its own biology. What that biology may actually be is open to our conjecture but part of understanding it is merely to accept it. Those travellers went close to the swallow. They saw it in its middle state. Now we know that middle state not to be true. Yet the swallow is further away from most of us than ever. How can we know more and still be further away? How have we arrived at this remove? We must accept again that biology. We must open the backdoor and look up.

There is an idea in architecture called critical regionalism. In many ways it is a response to the homogenous main streets and high streets that now occupy our towns and cities and that are more a reflection of commercial imperatives than they are of anything else. Their context, like the supermarkets that bookend the town through which the bypass runs, is devoid of any geographical reality. Critical regionalism is in opposition to that. It sees the identity of a place as paramount to the form of the place. Our swallows could be the emblem of our critical regionalism. The bird that eschews all boundaries and which is, the swift aside, the most immediate example of a bird outside our parameters, whose pastures are the fields of the sky, is the most potent symbol of locality. It denotes both the time and the place, the season and the year. On a summer's evening it is the most gregarious and vociferous. In the winter it is present by its absence. If we are to talk truly of where we live, we have to talk of the swallow. The swallow could be our response.

These early April days as I turn my eyes to the sky and wait I am thinking again of last September when I walked in the yard and the birds drew patterns across the sky that I could not understand. To be honest, I wonder now was I trying to understand at all. From the red sky on the western horizon and the swirling movements of the crows and the sparrows I do not think I sought to investigate. I merely watched. In that moment two other moments came to my mind, two other sensations drew themselves towards the edge of my consciousness. For the first instance I was, there in the yard by the old farmhouse and the uneven acre, above the now silent traffic of the main Cork road, brought towards the pristine moment. I stood by a young apple tree and watched the birds moving across the sky and no other noise could be heard and no other movements broke across my vision. I felt for a fleeting moment as if the ice had just cleared, as if the vast waterways covered the island, as if the forests still stood. I felt for a brief instant as I stood upon the earth as if I had found, in this of all places, these few yards from my backdoor, the unmodified moment. I imagined for a moment, framed by the sky and the flying birds, something I will never see. Then I looked up and saw something that, for the briefest of moments, brought me full circle, back to another year and the cornfield off a bypass. Above the bottom yard, with the shabby outbuildings, swallows flew up and down. They fell from the sky. The noise of the summer months had gone but the birds remained. They moved across the sky, up and down, in silent patterns of movement. One moment forty-odd of them had lined the house roof. Now many more of them moved above the yard in that same silent dance of twelve months ago. They stopped. As quickly as I had stumbled upon it, it broke apart and the swallows were calling. Their incessant noise broke through again. The middle state had come to the yard and just as quickly the middle state was gone.

To become dwellers in the land . . . to come to know the earth, fully and honestly, the crucial and perhaps only and all-encompassing task is to understand the place, the immediate, specific place where we live.[1]

Kirkpatrick Sale

15

Coming Back

For the last three years at least the swallows have returned to the nest sites in this yard on exactly the same date, 12 April. Or should I say that I have observed them for the first time each year on that date. This year there are cold, northerly winds blowing down across the valley and across the fields, over the back of the house and out, out across the land towards the sea, from where the swallows will arrive. I wonder will these winds delay them. I wonder whether they will set out but then turn back when they meet this weather front blowing against them. I can look at the sky but have no way of knowing.

Waiting, I try to retrace my steps. I cycle down to the town and out along the bypass, past the silent cornfield and the new estate. I go out to the headland, following old footsteps I have made over the years, but that cold wind does not make me wish to stay on the narrow neck of land, the land beyond the near invisible outline of the fortified tower. Nothing lingers on the rocks to share my watch. I see no choughs. I sit a while beside the grotto, sheltered here from that cold wind and I taste the fresh chill of the water and savour the silence. I return one cold day to the burgeoning woods. The wind, still cold, comes in off the sea and the early trees do not yet break it up. I walk out through the other side of the wood and see the ocean before me. I wonder if, further along, the tough raven's nest is being used this early but do not feel I should disturb it. I glance out at the water, see the renowned headland over to the left. No small bodies of migrant birds make their way above those waves. None that I can see. I walk the lane, the sweet gorse in flower. I look out across the enduring fields. One side of the lane has been cut back and reveals a surviving body of old stone wall. The hands and the lives of that wall are gone. The stone is still there. I walk back along the lane and then cycle down to the disused quarry, the lanes dropping down to the sea. No peregrine sits on the ledge. I climb a rickety gate that the council have installed and make my way across the broken ground. Amongst the outsized slabs of rock is a scattering of skulls that appear to be those of jackdaws. I look up and a few crow-black birds fly above the heather-covered cliff.

One cold morning I go to the Mass rock. The well there is full but the stone steps are dry. I stand a while in the secret place. That cold evening I stand in the yard but no blackbird sings and as I walk away I hear it chittering, nervously, complainingly, from a bush. Another cold, shrouded morning, I go to the lagoon where the otters swam. The birds are asleep on the water. I see a fox making its way along the side of the road. The morning clears and the birds wake quickly and begin to move. That same afternoon, as the days of April gather on, I go again to the headland. The wind is less. Birds are out again on the rocks. Gulls fly to and fro across the water, patterns of movement I again only vaguely discern. Cormorants fly low above the dark waves. I stay longer this time but the lengthening day is still short. I watch a while from the rocks but no seal appears and there is now no seal in this book. I am in the yard again and it would be hard not to notice that the messy, urban starlings have returned and are nesting again beneath the corrugated roof. They are shy but busy. My city birds are with me again. There are jackdaws too, of course, nesting in the chimney. I can see them just above the rim of the chimney itself. In the morning their noise is the sound of this place. One day soon afterwards, I am in the town and I look up at the high steeples of the church but there are no swifts yet; they are some of the last to arrive and some of the first to leave. They are the great wonder, the great unknown, the great familiar, the great contradiction. I watch the sky. I watch the weather.

At the end of summer, for days after I had seen a small display of the middle state above the yard, I noticed how the earth around me had changed. There was a silence. Swallows that had for weeks screamed with a growing intensity, as if the excitement of departure was upon them, suddenly grew quiet. Many disappeared as the days went on but numbers of them still flew around the fields, above the yard, just when I thought they had gone. I wondered as I watched them whether the fledgling swallow I had seen perched on the old outbuilding door was amongst them. That bird had made its way finally out of the outhouse and I was convinced I was watching its first flight. It had sat on the door for a while watching the earth around it. Above it the sky was filled with the screams of other swallows. The bird glanced up, once, twice. It looked up again and took to the air and in a moment it was gone into the swirl of birds above. I had watched its first flight into the air and soon it would be preparing to fly across Europe and the Sahara and the rainforest and land in southern Africa. One day above the front of the house a kestrel hovered, poised perfectly. Swallows flew nearby but did not scream and mob the small raptor as they had done days before. There was a sense of stillness emanating outwards from the kestrel. There was quiet in the sky. For a moment the world the kestrel sees, as it hovers so far above it, came tantalisingly close. For a little while there was only the kestrel and the air. The swallows remained for days to come but their screaming intensity had already departed. The middle state was in the air. I went one cold morning to bring wood from the outhouse. A thought came to me and I went around to the old stable, the corrugated roof with a few more holes every year. I pushed against the gate just inside the door and saw the crack. The creak sounded and it was the height of summer again and I was lifting children up to see the swallow nest and the swallow eggs, the chicks, the fledglings. I recalled that those days of silent movement in the air, those autumn days before the birds left, those days of the middle state, are thought to constitute for the young birds a time when they disperse around the area in order to get to know it. They do not inherit the geographical information of their locality and so those days of wandering are their grounding in their own bioregion, their learning of their own summer space, their journeying around the backdoor.

I think on the end of summer again as I wait, as if it is the return of summer itself that the swallows will bring with them. I recall the sudden cool of September, checking the outhouses in the yard in the evenings and still finding swallows roosting there on the beams, the last of the summer broods perhaps, the migration so soon ahead of them. I recall the odd mix of starlings and swallows on the wires and flying above the yard in the evenings, too. The soporific, melancholy sound of woodpigeons in the motionless green trees. Of the gathering crows, the rooks and the jackdaws, flocks still small by winter standards, flying overhead as I watched and then turning to fly back over my head and the roof of the house, low in the autumn sky, so low that I could hear their movement, their calls, the beating of their wings. I could hear flying.

So many times in this book I have discovered company when I did not expect it and so many times I have found myself back again at some kind of beginning. One morning the beginning itself returns. After the long months of winter and the cold days of spring there is a familiar shape in the sky. I have waited for this and whilst I waited, tried to discover as much as possible. Now there is a completeness. I look up at the sky for a final time. There is a swallow above the yard. They have returned.

Endnotes

Introduction

1. Patrick Kavanagh, *Kavanagh's Weekly* (Dublin, 24 May 1952).
2. Robert Lloyd Praeger, *The Way that I Went* (Dublin, 1969), p. 2.
3. Jonathan Bate, *The Song of the Earth* (London, 2000), p. 23.

Chapter 1: The Middle State

1. Richard Louv, *Last Child in the Woods – Saving Our Children From Nature Deficit Disorder* (New York, 2005), p. 180.
2. John Wilson Foster, *Nature in Ireland – A Scientific and Cultural History* (Dublin, 1998), p. 43.
3. *Ibid.*, p. 43.
4. Arthur Quiller-Couch, *The Oxford Book of English Verse 1250–1900* (Oxford, 1927), p. 112.
5. Brian Friel, *Translations* (London, 1981), p. 63.
6. Cathal Póirtéir, *Famine Echoes* (Dublin, 1995), p. 17.
7. Tim Robinson, *A Map of the Aran Islands* (Roundstone, 1996).
8. John Montague, *The Shop Magazine* (Schull, 2002), p. 7.
9. Patrick Duffy, *Exploring The History and Heritage of Irish Landscapes* (Dublin, 2007), p. 13.
10. Wilson Foster, *op. cit.*, p. 24.
11. *Ibid.*, p. 24.
12. K. H. Jackson, *A Celtic Miscellany* (London, 1971), p. 87.
13. *Encyclopaedia of Birds Vol. 2* (London, *c.* 1980), p. 234.
14. P. A. D. Hollom, *The Popular Handbook of British Birds* (Gateshead, 1962), p. 166.

15. E. M. Nicholson, *Birds and Men* (London, 1990), p. 85.
16. Tony Soper, *Everyday Birds* (Oxford, 1976), p. 89.
17. David Cabot, *Ireland* (London, 1999), p. 20.
18. *Ibid.*, p. 20.
19. Wilson Foster, *op. cit.*, p. 45.

Chapter 2: Desire Paths

1. Patrick Duffy, *Exploring the History and Heritage of Irish Landscapes* (Dublin, 2007), p. 13.
2. *Ibid.*, p. 15.
3. Keogh, O'Shea & Quinlan, *Ireland in the 1950s: The Lost Decade* (Cork, 2004), p. 22.
4. David Cabot, *Ireland* (London, 1999), p. 11.
5. Robert Welch, *Oxford Companion to Irish Literature* (Oxford, 2000) p. R.
6. Duffy, *op. cit.*, p. 103.
7. Duffy, *op. cit.*, p. 102.
8. John Wilson Foster, *Nature in Ireland – A Scientific and Cultural History* (Dublin, 1998), p. 24.
9. T. Hayden & R. Harrington, *Exploring Irish Mammals* (Dublin, 2000), p. 99.
10. Michael J. Carroll, *The Castles and Fortified Houses of West Cork* (Bantry, 2001), p. 113.
11. Duffy, *op. cit.*, p. 225.
12. Wilson Foster, *op. cit.*, p. 81.
13. Aidan Mathews, *Minding Ruth* (Oldcastle, 1983), p. 24.
14. Michael Viney, *Irish Review I* (Dublin, 1986), pp. 58–64.
15. Dempsey & O'Clery, *The Complete Guide to Ireland's Birds* (Dublin, 2002), p. 208.
16. Wilson Foster, *op. cit.*, p. 453.
17. Damien Enright, *Walks of Courtmacsherry Bay & The Seven Heads* (Timoleague, 1998), p. 39.

Chapter 3: The Fifth Element

1. Roger Deakin, *Wildwood: A Journey through Trees* (London, 2007), p. ix.
2. Damien Enright, *Walks of Courtmacsherry Bay & The Seven Heads* (Timoleague, 1998), p. 37.
3. Deakin, *op. cit.*, p. x.
4. Jean Giono, *The Man Who Planted Trees* (London, 1989), p. 49.
5. André Comte-Sponville, *A Short Treatise on the Great Virtues* (London, 2003), p. 149.

6. Frank Mitchell & Michael Ryan, *Reading the Irish Landscape* (Dublin, 1997), p. 144.
7. John Wilson Foster, *Nature in Ireland – A Scientific and Cultural History* (Dublin, 1998), p. 136.
8. R. F. Foster, *Modern Ireland 1600–1972* (London, 1989), p. 6.
9. Wilson Foster, *op. cit.*, p. 141.
10. Daniel Corkery, *The Hidden Ireland* (Dublin, 1967), p. 36.
11. David Dickson, *Old World Colony* (Cork, 2005), p. 227.
12. David Hickie, *Native Trees & Forests of Ireland* (Dublin, 2002), p. 6.
13. Corkery, *op. cit.*, p. 34.
14. Declan Kiberd, *Irish Classics* (London, 2000), p. 80.
15. Seán Ó Tuama & Thomas Kinsella, *An Duanaire 1600–1900: Poems of the Dispossessed* (Portlaoise, 1981), p. 328.
16. Wilson Foster, *op. cit.*, p. 140.
17. Wilson Foster, *op. cit.*, p. 150.
18. Austin Clarke, *Collected Poems* (Manchester, 2008), p. 169.
19. Dickson; *op. cit.*, p. 20.
20. Wilson Foster, *op. cit.*, p. 550.
21. Wilson Foster, *op. cit.*, p. 552.
22. Wilson Foster, *op. cit.*, p. 556.
23. Jeremy Sandford, *Mary Carbery's West Cork Journal 1898–1901* (Dublin, 1998), p. 18.
24. Sylvia Bruce Wilmore, *Crows, Jays, Ravens* (London, 1977), p. 19.
25. *Ibid.*, p. 150.
26. John Clare, *Selected Poems* (London, 2000), p. 103.

Chapter 4: Perception's Pace

1. Robert Lloyd Praeger, *The Way that I Went* (Dublin, 1969), p. 2.
2. John Montague, *Selected Poems* (London, 2001), p. 174.
3. Henry Thoreau, *Walking* (Maryland, 2007), pp. 7–8.
4. Sean Sheehan, *Jack's World* (Youghal, 2007), p. 3.
5. Liam De Paor (ed.), *Milestones in Irish History* (Cork, 1998), p. 106.
6. *Ibid.*, p. 107.
7. Patrick Duffy, *Exploring the History and Heritage of Irish Landscapes* (Dublin, 2007), p. 20.
8. Duffy, *op. cit.*, p. 20.
9. Simon Schama, *Landscape and Memory* (London, 1995), p. 574.
10. Michael Fewer, *A Walk in Ireland* (Cork, 2001), p. 222.

11. Lloyd Praeger, *op. cit.*, p. 22.

12. William Cobbett, *Rural Rides* (Exeter, 1984), p. 171.

13. Louis MacNeice, *Collected Poems* (London, 1986), p. 30.

14. John Wilson Foster, *Nature in Ireland – A Scientific and Cultural History* (Dublin, 1998), p. 420.

15. Wilson Foster, *op. cit.*, p. 274.

16. Wilson Foster, *op. cit.*, p. 503.

17. Lloyd Praeger, *op. cit.*, p. 1.

18. Henry Thoreau, *Walden* (London, 1938), p. 97.

Chapter 5: The Shared Experience

1. Gary Snyder, *The Practice of the Wild* (California, 1990), p. 7.

2. Lloyd Praeger, *The Way that I Went* (Dublin, 1969), p. 198.

3. Derek Ratcliffe, *The Peregrine* (Calton, 1980), p. 39.

4. Rachel Carson, *Silent Spring* (London, 1999), p. 118.

5. *Ibid.*, p. 13.

6. *Ibid.*, p. 118.

7. Barry Lopez, *Of Wolves and Men* (New York, 1995), pp. 179–180.

8. Flann O'Brien, *The Third Policeman* (London, 1974), p. 72.

9. Antoinette Quinn, *Patrick Kavanagh – A Biography* (Dublin, 2003), p. 43.

10. Patrick Kavanagh, *Selected Poems* (London, 1996), p. 6.

11. Micheal Briody, *The Irish Folklore Commission 1935–1970* (Helsinki, 2007), p. 246.

12. Charles Townshend, *Easter 1916: The Irish Rebellion* (London, 2006), p. 82.

13. Carson, *op. cit.*, p. 258.

14. John Wilson Foster, *Nature in Ireland – A Scientific and Cultural History* (Dublin, 1998), p. 605.

15. Oscar Wilde, *De Profundis* (London, c. 1930), p. 109.

16. Gordon D'Arcy, *Ireland's Lost Birds* (Dublin, 2000), p. 124.

17. *Ibid.*, p. 124.

18. *Ibid.*, p. 124.

19. Mark Cocker & Richard Mabey, *Birds Britannica* (London, 2005), p. 166.

20. Snyder, *op. cit.*, p. 101.

21. Richard Mabey, *Nature Cure* (London, 2005), p. 103.

22. Snyder, *op. cit.*, p. 106.

23. Wilson Foster, *op. cit.*, p. 493.

24. R. Ussher & R. Warren: *Birds of Ireland* (London, 1900), p. 138.

25. *Ibid.*, p. 141.

26. *Ibid.*, p. 138.

27. Clive D. Hutchinson, *Birds in Ireland* (Calton, 1989), p. 92.

28. D'Arcy, *op. cit.*, p. 29.

Chapter 6: The Backyard and the Song

1. J. Aitchison, *The Articulate Mammal: An Introduction into Psycholinguistics* (New York, 1998), p. 104.

2. Mark Cocker & Richard Mabey, *Birds Britannica* (London, 2005), p. 328.

3. *Ibid.*, p. 328.

4. Gary Snyder, *The Practice of the Wild* (California, 1990), p. 92.

5. *Ibid.*, p. 19.

6. Patricia Craig, *The Oxford Book of Ireland* (Oxford, 1998), p. 248.

7. Snyder, *op. cit.*, p. 101.

8. Snyder, *op. cit.*, p. 101.

9. Seamus Heaney, *History Ireland* (Dublin, 1993), p. 33.

10. Milan Kundera, *The Book of Laughter and Forgetting* (Calcutta, 1998), p. 3.

11. Cocker & Mabey, *op. cit.*, p. 351.

12. James Carney, *Early Irish Poetry* (Cork, 1969), p. 13.

13. John Montague (ed.), *The Faber Book of Irish Verse* (London, 1978), p. 23.

14. *Ibid.*, p. 58.

15. *Ibid.*, p. 80.

16. *Ibid.*, p. 82.

17. Seán Ó Tuama & Thomas Kinsella (eds.), *An Duanaire 1600–1900: Poems of the Dispossessed* (Portlaoise, 1981), p. 41.

18. Thomas Kinsella (ed.), *The New Oxford Book of Irish Verse* (Oxford, 1991), p. 30.

19. Snyder, *op. cit.*, p. 101.

20. Montague (ed.), *op. cit.*, p. 56.

21. Francis Ledwidge, *Complete Poems* (London, 1995), p. 43.

22. Seamus Heaney, *District and Circle* (London, 2006), p. 75.

Chapter 7: The Unsophisticated Spot

1. Richard Jeffries, *The Story of My Heart* (London, 1938), p. 20.

2. Gordon D'Arcy, *Ireland's Lost Birds* (Dublin, 2000), p. 25.

3. Jonathan Pilcher & Valerie Hall, *Flora Hibernica* (Cork, 2001), p. 4.

4. *Ibid.*, p. 4.

5. Michael Viney, *Ireland* (Belfast, 2003), p. 58.

6. John Wilson Foster, *Nature in Ireland* (Dublin, 1998), p. 170.

7. Ellen Hutchins & Dawson Turner, *Early Observations on the Flora of South*

West Ireland (Dublin, 1999), p. 20.

8. *Ibid.*, pp. 32–33.

9. Michael Viney, *A Year's Turning* (London, 1998), p. 15.

10. *Ibid.*, p.15.

11. Damien Enright, *Walks of Clonakilty Town and Country* (Timoleague, 1999), p. 32.

12. Rainer Maria Rilke, *Selected Poems* (London, 2000), p. 21.

13. *Ibid.*, p. 21.

14. *Ibid.*, p. 21.

15. Seamus Heaney, *New Selected Poems* (London, 1990), p. 120.

Chapter 8: No Beginning and No End

1. Rachel Carson, *Silent Spring* (London, 1999), p. 24.

2. John Montague (ed.), *The Faber Book of Irish Verse* (London, 1978), p. 60.

3. Jeremy Sandford, *Mary Carbery's West Cork Journal 1898–1901* (Dublin, 1998), p. 87.

4. P. J. Kavanagh, *Voices in Ireland* (London, 1995), p. 181.

5. Seamus Heaney, *New Selected Poems* (London, 1990), p. 115.

6. Chet Raymo, *Honey from Stone* (Dingle, 1997), p. 109.

7. Jonathan Pilcher & Valerie Hall, *Flora Hibernica* (Cork, 2001), p. 50.

8. Mark Cocker & Richard Mabey, *Birds Britannica*, (London, 2005), p. 424.

9. John Keats, *Selected Poems* (London, 1953), p. 50.

10. Gerard Manley Hopkins, *Selected Poetry* (Oxford, 1998), p. 117.

11. Matthew Arnold, *Selected Poems and Prose* (London, 1991), p. 88.

12. Frank Mitchell & Michael Ryan, *Reading the Irish Landscape* (Dublin, 1997), p. 14.

13. *Ibid.*, p. 20.

14. Walt Whitman, *Leaves of Grass* (London, 1986), p. 25.

15. Mitchell & Ryan, *op. cit.*, p. 1.

Chapter 9: Native Fishermen

1. David Thomson, *The People of the Sea* (London, 1980), p. 12.

2. Thomas Kinsella (ed.), *The New Oxford Book of Irish Verse* (Oxford, 1991), p. 125.

3. Jonathan Bate, *The Song of the Earth*, (London, 2000), p. 74.

4. Declan Kiberd, *Irish Classics* (London, 2000), p. 21.

5. *Ibid.*, p. 3.

6. Thomson, *op. cit.*, p. 11.

7. Thomson, *op. cit.*, p. 86.

8. Kinsella (ed.), *op. cit*, p. 46.
9. Kennedy, Ell, Crawford & Clarkson, *Mapping The Great Irish Famine* (Dublin, 1999), p. 75.
10. Cecil Woodham-Smith, *The Great Hunger* (London, 1963), p. 289.
11. Thomson, *op. cit.*, p. 13.
12. Thomson, *op. cit.*, p. 145.
13. Thomson, *op. cit.*, p. 94.
14. Thomson, *op. cit.*, p. 94.
15. Thomson, *op. cit.*, p. 13.

Chapter 10: A Murmuration

1. Roy Fisher, *A Furnace* (Oxford, 1986), p. 1.
2. Mark Cocker & Richard Mabey, *Birds Britannica* (London, 2005), p. 429.
3. *Ibid.*, p. 432.
4. *Ibid.*, p. 432.
5. Patrick Duffy, *Exploring the History and Heritage of Irish Landscapes* (Dublin, 2007), p. 124.
6. *Ibid.*, p. 20.
7. *Ibid.*, p. 115.
8. *Ibid.*, p. 126.
9. Tony Soper, *Everyday Birds* (Oxford, 1976), p. 54.
10. Cocker & Mabey, *op. cit.*, p. 433.
11. Cocker & Mabey, *op. cit.*, p. 441.
12. Aldo Leopold, *A Sand Country Almanac* (New York, 1968), p. 174.
13. Roy Fisher, *Birmingham River* (Oxford, 1994), p. 13.

Chapter 11: The Shape and the Testimony

1. Gary Snyder, *The Practice of the Wild* (California, 1990), p. 69.
2. Patrick Duffy, *Exploring the History and Heritage of Irish Landscapes* (Dublin, 2007), p. 55.
3. Peter Somerville-Large, *Irish Voices* (London, 1999), p. 81.
4. Duffy, *op. cit.*, p. 45.
5. John Clare, *Selected Poems* (London, 2000), p. 198.
6. *Ibid.*, p. 169.
7. Jonathan Bate, *The Song of the Earth* (London, 2000), p. 162.
8. *Ibid.*, p. 166.
9. *Ibid.*, p. 173.
10. John Wilson Foster, *Nature in Ireland – A Scientific and Cultural History*

(Dublin, 1998), p. 419.

11. *Ibid.*, p. 419.

12. Patrick Kavanagh, *Collected Poems* (London, 2004), p. 38.

13. *Ibid.*, p. 200.

14. Simon Schama, *Landscape and Memory* (London, 1995), p. 7.

15. *Ibid.*, p. 61.

16. Wilson Foster, *op. cit.*, p. 440.

17. Wilson Foster, *op. cit.*, p. 441.

18. Wilson Foster, *op. cit.*, p. 445.

19. Seamus Heaney, *Door into the Dark* (London, 1969), p. 21.

20. B. Devall & G. Sessions, *Deep Ecology* (Utah, 1985), p. 66.

21. Aldo Leopold, *A Sand Country Almanac* (New York, 1968), p. 20.

22. Wilson Foster, *op. cit.*, p. 443.

23. Bate, *op. cit.*, p. 237.

24. Richard Mabey, *Nature Cure* (London, 2005), p. 93.

25. Mark Cocker & Richard Mabey, *Birds Britannica* (London, 2005), p. 410.

26. Sylvia Bruce Wilmore, *Crows, Jays, Ravens* (London, 1977), p. 174.

27. *Ibid.*, p. 176.

28. Mark Cocker, *Crow Country* (London, 2007), p. 136.

29. Bruce Wilmore, *op. cit.*, p. 134.

30. Cocker, *op. cit.*, p. 412.

31. Bruce Wilmore, *op. cit.*, p. 179.

Chapter 12: As if the Bow Had Flown Off . . .

1. J. A. Baker, *The Peregrine* (London, 1976), p. 13.

2. Gilbert White, *The Natural History of Selborne* (London, 1902), p. 185.

3. *Encyclopaedia of Birds Vol. 4* (London, *c.* 1980), p. 70.

4. Richard Mabey, *Nature Cure* (London, 2005), p. 172.

5. White, *op. cit.*, p. xv.

6. White, *op. cit.*, p. 185.

7. E. M. Nicholson, *Birds and Men* (London, 1990), p. 215.

8. W. D. Campbell, *Birds of Town and Village* (London, 1965), p. 109.

9. Mark Cocker & Richard Mabey, *Birds Britannica* (London, 2005), p. 298.

10. *Encyclopaedia of Birds Vol. 4* (London, *c.* 1980), p. 72.

11. Nicholson, *op. cit.*, p. 215.

12. Carl-Fredrik Lundevall, *The British Ornithologists' Guide to Bird Life* (Poole, 1980), p. 234.

13. Dominic Couzens, *Bird Migration* (London, 2005), p. 69.

14. Nicholson, *op. cit.*, p. 219.

15. Cocker & Mabey, *op. cit.*, p. 297.
16. Edward Thomas, *Collected Poems* (London, 2004), p. 81.

Chapter 13: Arguing with an April Wind

1. Jonathan Bate, *The Song of the Earth* (London, 2000), p. 114.
2. Trish Howley & Sandra Landers, *Weather Watch* (Tralee, 2008), p. 64.
3. John Wilson Foster, *Nature in Ireland* (Dublin, 1998), p. 446.
4. Chet Raymo, *Honey from Stone* (Dingle, 1997), p. 39.
5. *Ibid.*, p. 46.
6. Wilson Foster, *op. cit.*, p. 129.
7. Michael Viney, *Ireland* (Belfast, 2003), p. 68.
8. Dominic Couzens, *Bird Migration* (London, 2005), p. 74.
9. Raymo, *op. cit.*, p. 49.
10. Angela Leighton, *On Form* (Oxford, 2008), p. 15.
11. Wilson Foster, *op. cit.*, p. 131.
12. Richard Mabey, *In a Green Shade* (London, 1985), p. 17.
13. Robert Lloyd Praeger, *The Way that I Went* (Dublin, 1969), p. 4.
14. Frank Mitchell & Michael Ryan, *Reading the Irish Landscape* (Dublin, 1997), p. 237.
15. Theobold Wolfe Tone, *History Ireland* (Dublin, 1996), p. 37.
16. Brendan McWilliams, *Weather Eye*, (Dublin, 2008), p. 133.
17. Cathal Póirtéir, *Famine Echoes* (Dublin, 1995), p. 41.
18. McWilliams, *op. cit.*, p. 191.

Chapter 14: As Much About Books

1. Jonathan Bate, *The Song of the Earth* (London, 2000), p. 161.
2. Seamus Heaney, *Preoccupations* (London, 1984), p. 131.
3. *Ibid.*, p. 181.
4. Simon Schama, *Landscape and Memory* (London, 1995), p. 7.
5. *Ibid.*, p. 9.
6. *Ibid.* p. 19.
7. *Ibid.*, p. 10.
8. Patrick Duffy, *Exploring the History and Heritage of Irish Landscapes* (Dublin, 2007), p. 13.
9. Gary Snyder, *Practice of the Wild* (California, 1990), p. 37.
10. Bate, *op. cit.*, p. 92.
11. Bate, *op. cit.*, p. 73.
12. Bate, *op. cit.*, p. 18.

13. W. B. Yeats, *The Poems* (London, 1992), p. 293.
14. Seamus Heaney, *Wintering Out* (London, 1972), p. 35.
15. Rachel Carson, *Silent Spring* (London, 1999), p. 261.
16. *Ibid.*, p. 261.
17. *Ibid.*, p. 100.
18. Bate, *op. cit.*, p. 231.
19. Carson, *op. cit.*, p. 107.
20. Carson, *op. cit.*, p. 121.
21. Bate, *op. cit.*, p. 151.
22. David Thomson, *The People of the Sea* (London, 1980), p. 11.
23. Bate, *op. cit.*, p. 235.
24. Bate, *op. cit.*, p. 264.
25. Charles Dixon, *The Migration of Birds* (London, 1892), p. 8.
26. *Ibid.*, p. 9.

Chapter 15: Coming Home

1. Kirkpatrick Sale, *Dwellers in the Land: The Bioregional Vision* (Atlanta, 2000), p. 42.

Bibliography

Aitchison, J., *The Articulate Mammal: An Introduction into Psycholinguistics* (New York, 1998)

Arnold, Mathew (Miriam Allott, ed.), *Selected Poems and Prose* (London, 1991)

Baker, J. A., *The Peregrine* (London, 1976)

Bate, Jonathan, *The Song of the Earth* (London, 2000)

Briody, Micheal, *The Irish Folklore Commission 1935–1970* (Helsinki 2007)

Bruce Wilmore, Sylvia, *Crows, Jays, Ravens* (London, 1977)

Cabot, David, *Ireland* (London, 1999)

Campbell, W. D., *Birds of Town and Village* (London, 1965)

Carney, James, *Early Irish Poetry* (Cork, 1969)

Carroll, Michael J., *The Castles and Fortified Houses of West Cork* (Bantry, 2001)

Carson, Rachel, *Silent Spring* (London, 1999)

Clare, John, *Selected Poems* (London, 2000)

Clarke, Austin, *Collected Poems* (Manchester, 2008)

Cobbett, William, *Rural Rides* (Exeter, 1984)

Cocker, Mark, & Mabey, Richard, *Birds Britannica* (London, 2005)

Cocker, Mark, *Crow Country* (London, 2007)

Comte-Sponville, André, *A Short Treatise on the Great Virtues* (London, 2003)

Corkery, Daniel, *The Hidden Ireland* (Dublin, 1967)

Couzens, Dominic, *Bird Migration* (London, 2005)

Craig, Patricia, *The Oxford Book of Ireland* (Oxford, 1998)

D'Arcy, Gordon, *Ireland's Lost Birds* (Dublin, 2000)

De Paor, Liam (ed.), *Milestones in Irish History* (Cork, 1998)

Bibliography

Deakin, Roger, *Wildwood: A Journey through Trees* (London, 2007)

Dempsey & O'Clery, *The Complete Guide to Ireland's Birds* (Dublin, 2002)

Devall, B. & Sessions, G., *Deep Ecology* (Utah, 1985)

Dickson, David, *Old World Colony* (Cork, 2005)

Dixon, Charles, *The Migration of Birds* (London, 1892)

Duffy, Patrick, *Exploring The History And Heritage Of Irish Landscapes* (Dublin, 2007)

Encyclopaedia Of Birds Vol. 2 (London)

Encyclopaedia Of Birds Vol. 4 (London)

Enright, Damien, *Walks of Courtmacsherry Bay & The Seven Heads* (Timoleague, 1998)

— *Walks of Clonakilty Town and Country* (Timoleague, 1999)

Fewer, Michael, *A Walk in Ireland* (Cork, 2001)

Fisher, Roy, *A Furnace* (Oxford, 1986)

— *Birmingham River* (Oxford, 1994)

Foster, R. F., *Modern Ireland 1600–1972* (London, 1989)

Friel, Brian, *Translations* (London, 1981)

Giono, Jean, *The Man Who Planted Trees* (London, 1989)

Hayden, T. & Harrington R., *Exploring Irish Mammals* (Dublin, 2000)

Heaney, Seamus, *Door into the Dark* (London, 1969)

— *Wintering Out* (London, 1972)

— *Preoccupations* (London, 1984)

— *New Selected Poems* (London, 1990)

— *History Ireland* (Dublin, Winter 1993)

— *District and Circle* (London, 2006)

Hickie, David, *Native Trees & Forests of Ireland* (Dublin, 2002)

Hollom, P. A. D., *The Popular Handbook of British Birds* (Gateshead, 1962)

Hopkins, Gerard Manley, *Selected Poetry* (Oxford, 1998)

Howley, Trish & Landers Sandra, *Weather Watch* (Tralee, 2008)

Hutchins, Ellen & Turner, Dawson, *Early Observations on the Flora of South West Ireland* (Dublin, 1999)

Hutchinson, Clive D., *Birds in Ireland* (Calton, 1989)

Jackson, K. H., *A Celtic Miscellany* (London, 1971)

Jeffries, Richard, *The Story of My Heart* (London, 1938)

Kavanagh, Patrick, *Kavanagh's Weekly*, (Dublin, 24 May 1952)

— *Voices in Ireland* (London, 1995)

— *Selected Poems* (London, 1996)

— *Collected Poems* (London, 2004)

Keats, John, *Selected Poems* (London, 1953)

Kennedy, Ell, Crawford & Clarkson, *Mapping The Great Irish Famine* (Dublin, 1999)

Keogh, O'Shea & Quinlan, *Ireland in the 1950s: The Lost Decade* (Cork, 2004)

Kiberd, Declan, *Irish Classics* (London, 2000)

Kinsella, Thomas (ed.), *The New Oxford Book of Irish Verse* (Oxford, 1991)

Kundera, Milan, *The Book of Laughter and Forgetting* (Calcutta, 1998)

Ledwidge, Francis, *Complete Poems* (London, 1995)

Leighton, Angela, *On Form* (Oxford, 2008)

Leopold, Aldo, *A Sand Country Almanac* (New York, 1968)

Lloyd Praeger, Robert, *The Way that I Went* (Dublin, 1969)

Lopez, Barry, *Of Wolves and Men* (New York, 1995)

Louv, Richard, *Last Child In The Woods – Saving Our Children From Nature Deficit Disorder* (New York, 2005)

Lundevall, Carl-Fredrik, *The British Ornithologists' Guide to Bird Life* (Poole, 1980)

Mabey, Richard, *In a Green Shade* (London, 1985)

— *Nature Cure* (London, 2005)

MacNeice, Louis, *Collected Poems* (London, 1986)

McWilliams, Brendan, *Weather Eye* (Dublin, 2008)

Mathews, Aidan, *Minding Ruth* (Oldcastle, 1983)

Mitchell, Frank & Ryan, Michael, *Reading the Irish Landscape* (Dublin, 1997)

Montague, John, (ed.), *The Faber Book of Irish Verse* (London, 1978)

— *Selected Poems* (London, 2001)

— *The Shop Magazine* (Schull, 2002)

Nicholson, E. M., *Birds and Men* (London, 1990)

O'Brien, Flann, *The Third Policeman* (London, 1974)

Ó Tuama, Seán & Kinsella, Thomas, *An Duanaire 1600–1900: Poems of the Dispossessed* (Portlaoise, 1981)

Pilcher, Jonathan & Hall, Valerie, *Flora Hibernica* (Cork, 2001)

Póirtéir, Cathal, *Famine Echoes* (Dublin, 1995)

Quiller-Couch, Arthur, *The Oxford Book of English Verse 1250–1900* (Oxford, 1927)

Quinn, Antoinette, *Patrick Kavanagh – A Biography* (Dublin, 2003)

Ratcliffe, Derek, *The Peregrine Falcon* (Calton, 1980)

Raymo, Chet, *Honey from Stone* (Dingle, 1997)

Rilke, Rainer Maria, *Selected Poems* (London, 2000)

Robinson, Tim, *A Map of the Aran Islands* (Roundstone, 1996)

Sale, Kirkpatrick, *Dwellers in the Land: The Bioregional Vision* (Atlanta, 2000)

Bibliography

Sandford, Jeremy, *Mary Carbery's West Cork Journal 1898–1901* (Dublin, 1998)

Schama, Simon, *Landscape and Memory* (London, 1995)

Sheehan, Seán, *Jack's World* (Youghal, 2007)

Snyder, Gary, *The Practice of the Wild* (California, 1990)

Somerville-Large, Peter, *Irish Voices* (London, 1999)

Soper, Tony, *Everyday Birds* (Oxford, 1976)

Thomas, Edward, *Collected Poems* (London, 2004)

Thomson, David, *The People of the Sea* (London, 1980)

Thoreau, Henry, *Walden* (London, 1938)

— *Walking* (Maryland, 2007)

Townshend, Charles, *Easter 1916: The Irish Rebellion* (London, 2006)

Ussher, R. & Warren, R., *Birds of Ireland* (London, 1900)

Viney, Michael, *Irish Review I* (Dublin, 1986)

— *A Year's Turning* (London, 1998)

— *Ireland* (Belfast, 2003)

Welch, Robert, *Oxford Companion to Irish Literature* (Oxford, 2000)

Wilde, Oscar, *De Profundis* (London, c. 1930)

White, Gilbert, *The Natural History of Selborne* (London, 1902)

Whitman, Walt, *Leaves of Grass* (London, 1986)

Wilson Foster, John, *Nature in Ireland – A Scientific and Cultural History* (Dublin, 1998)

Woodham-Smith, Cecil, *The Great Hunger* (London, 1963)

Yeats, W. B., *The Poems* (London, 1992)

JOSEPH HORGAN, born in England, came to live in Ireland in 1999. Shortlisted for the Hennessy Award for New Irish Writing in 2003, in 2004 he was awarded the Patrick Kavanagh award for poetry. His work has been broadcast on RTÉ radio and television and he writes a weekly column for the *Irish Post*. His poetry has been published in various journals and his first collection, *Slipping Letters Beneath the Sea*, was published in 2008. He lives in County Cork with his wife and their three children.